D0185776

# TILLY'S KITCHEN TAKEOVER

# Matilda and the Ramsay bunch

# TILLY'S KITCHEN TAKEOVER

## MATILDA RAMSAY

HODDER & STOUGHTON

# CONTENTS

Here's the whole of the Ramsay gang hanging out in our favourite room of the house: the kitchen!

# CHEF TO CHEF

Did you know that Tilly was born on my birthday? Perhaps it was inevitable, then, that she would be the only one of my four children to follow in my footsteps. I think it is absolutely brilliant that my youngest daughter is so into cooking and that she wants to teach other people, too. She learnt to use a chef's knife when she was six and is a total natural in the kitchen. And in front of the camera for that matter. One day, I know her ratings are going to beat mine, but don't tell her I said that . . .

Apparently Tilly finds me really annoying in the kitchen. Personally, I don't see why . . . Doesn't she see that I'm just trying to help? She's pretty good at cooking but I'm the one with the 30 plus years of experience, the Michelin stars, the restaurants all round the world . . . You'd think she'd be happy to learn from the master! But she says my food is too fancy and that she cooks 'real' food. I suppose I see her point – all the recipes in this book are pretty uncomplicated while still producing really delicious results. I've added a few tips of my own to help you along the way though. Not that I'm interfering or anything.

Tilly definitely has all the makings of a great chef. She works hard, is really talented (I take some of the credit for that, obviously) and she loves good food. She might think I'm getting in the way and being critical but what I really am is a very proud dad. She makes cooking look like a lot of fun and consistently produces really good food. She's amazing. In fact, I'm tempted to give her and this great book a whopping ten out of ten. Well done, Tilly!

*Gordon x*

THANKS, DAD!

HI, MY NAME'S MATILDA

BUT MOST PEOPLE JUST CALL ME TILLY

I love cooking up a storm for my crazy family when we are on holiday in L.A. and Cornwall and back home where we live in London. I'm super lucky because my parents let me take over the kitchen whenever I want and I love trying out new things, making a mess and producing really delicious food. It can be really mad filming my TV programme but it's also brilliant fun because we get to do all sorts of amazing things together as a family and we meet so many great people. For me, the food is definitely the best part, though.

My dad is *quite* a good cook . . . actually, he's a proper chef who's famous for bossing people about on TV. In real life, he's not nearly so shouty and I love talking to him about food. He does try to take over in the kitchen, which can be annoying, but mostly it's really fun and he teaches me so much. I don't cook posh, fancy pants food like he does but he still likes to taste everything I make. He can be quite critical but I think that's a good thing because it helps me get better. Once he gave me a ten out of ten for my magic ice cream (see page 197) which was totally awesome!

I have learnt a lot about cooking from dad but I have also learnt a lot from mum who's a brilliant cook, too. In fact, she actually cooks the most at home and she's the one who has taught me all the basics. Her spaghetti Bolognese is definitely my desert island meal – I could eat it almost every day! Mum really loves healthy food and has introduced us to chia seeds, green smoothies and kale salads, among other tasty things. We're all happy to eat healthy food because mum makes meals that are so delicious you don't even realise they are good for you too! I'm really influenced by her in this way and am always looking for ways to give my not-so-healthy favourite dishes a fresh Tilly makeover.

Given that both of my parents are really into food and cooking, I suppose it isn't much of a surprise that I am crazy about it, too. Cooking makes me really happy. It's so creative and I love experimenting with new recipes and trying different combinations. I especially enjoy watching people tuck into the things I've cooked. It's such a great feeling.

This book is full of the yummy, easy food that I love cooking on the TV show and that I hope you will enjoy. I've tried to keep the recipes simple so that they are fun and don't take too long. Hopefully, you should be able to do most things yourself, with a little bit of help from your parents here and there. Whatever you do, don't get stressed – it's not the end of the world if something doesn't work out how you want it to. You just need to get stuck in and start cooking up your own storm! So, the big question is . . . What are you waiting for?

*Tilly Ramsay*

# TILLY'S RULES, OK?

Before you take over the kitchen, there are some rules you should know about. If you stick to these, you won't hurt yourself, make anyone sick or get your parents really cross (hopefully!).

✓ **1. Ask permission.** However good at cooking you are, mums and dads like to know what you are up to in the kitchen, especially when it involves sharp knives and hot pans. Always let them know before you get started . . . They might hang around in the background to watch over you but that's OK too – you might need their help from time to time.

✓ **2. Get ready.** Before you start cooking, always wash your hands and make sure your hair is off your face. If you are wearing light-coloured clothes or a favourite T-shirt, put on an apron to keep yourself clean.

✓ **3. Be careful of hot things.** Touching hot pans will burn and hurt like mad. The same goes for hot liquids and ingredients. Always use oven gloves when handling hot pans and keep your fingers away from flames, kettles, hot ovens, gas rings etc.

✓ **4. Be hygienic.** When you handle raw meat, eggs, shellfish and fish, you need to wash your hands before and after so you don't spread bacteria and other germs. Make sure you also clean anything that comes into contact with these raw ingredients like boards, bowls and knives.

✓ **5. Learn how to use a knife properly.** Knives are sharp and should be handled with extreme care. Learning how to hold one properly and how to chop with confidence will make using a knife much safer. See page 12 for some instructions.

✓ **6. Tidy up.** A good chef is a tidy chef. . . or so mum says. I am a disaster in the kitchen when it comes to mess but I always clean up after myself and I've found that my parents are much more keen for me to take over the kitchen if I leave it as I found it.

✓ **7. Have fun!** Dad always says that it really shows in the food if you have enjoyed cooking it, so don't get stressed: enjoy yourself!

# NEED TO KNOW

These are basic skills that you should try to master because you will come across them again and again. Knowing how to do these things will mean you can cook more and more recipes with confidence. Get practising!

## HOW TO USE A KNIFE

Learning to use a knife properly will mean you have the right skills to chop and slice things without hurting yourself. And the better you get at it, the more confident your parents will be to let you get on with the cooking, so practise whenever you can. Every time your mum or dad needs to chop an onion, offer to do it for them, and help with prepping vegetables with their guidance. Become the chief chopper in the house and you will get really good really quickly.

- If you aren't tall enough to chop something on the work top easily, either stand on a step or do your prepping at the kitchen table. You need to be at a comfortable height to chop things properly.

- Concentrate on what you are doing and cut slowly, especially when you are just starting to learn. You don't need to do super speedy slicing like a professional chef! Take your time.

- I know it doesn't sound right but the sharper your knife is, the safer it is – if your knife isn't sharp then it is more likely to slip when you're using it, which is when accidents happen. So make sure your knives are sharpened regularly – get mum or dad to help.

- Hold the knife in a relaxed but firm grip. Gripping too hard will stop your wrist and arm from moving naturally but if you don't grip it properly, you won't have any strength for slicing and chopping. Try different grips until you feel comfortable.

- When you are cutting vegetables etc., you always hold the vegetable steady with your free hand. So that you don't slice the tops off your fingers, keep them tucked under so that it is the nails that are holding the veg in place rather than the finger tips – it's just like making a claw with your hand. Always move the fingers away from the knife as you cut along the length of the veg so they are always at least 2cm away from the blade.

- When you have finished using the knife, always put it somewhere safe, away from the edge of the work top or table. Never put it into a sink full of washing up water – you could easily forget it is in there, and then you or someone else could really hurt themselves by putting their hand in the water.

## HOW TO CHOP AN ONION

- Chop the top off the onion then cut it in half down the middle through the root (step 1).
- Peel off the brown skin but leave the root (step 2).
- Put the onion halves cut-side down on to a sturdy chopping board and hold on to one of them firmly. Turn your knife flat and cut horizontally into the onion without going all the way through. Do this again a little bit higher (step 3).
- Turn your knife so the blade is facing down and make vertical slices from the root end to the top end. The root should keep the sliced onion half in one piece (step 4). Are you crying yet? Chopping onions can make your eyes really sore . . .
- Turn the onion 90 degrees so that the flat end is facing the knife and slice downwards several times until you reach the root which you can throw away (step 5). You should now have lots of little squares of onion (step 6). Repeat with the other half.

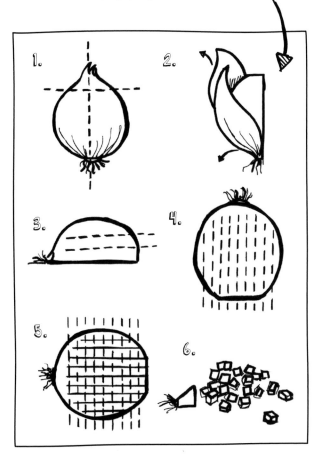

## HOW TO DESEED AND CHOP A CHILLI

- Cut the green top off, then, wearing rubber gloves, roll the chilli between your palms with the cut end over a plate or chopping board. As you roll the chilli back and forward, the seeds should fall out on to the plate or board. The heat of the chilli is in the seeds and white membrane, so keep them in if you like things hot!
- When you have got rid of all the seeds, cut the chilli in half lengthways and fold out the two halves so they are flat on the board, flesh side up.
- Use a teaspoon to scrape off any white membrane and throw it away.
- Hold on to the tip of one of the chilli halves and use a small paring knife to make slices from the tip to the top, but start just below the tip so that the slices are still connected to each other.
- Turn the chilli half 90 degrees and cut across the slices to give you small squares of chilli ready to add some fire to your food. Repeat with the other half.
- BE CAREFUL – don't touch your eyes or face while you are chopping chillies – it really stings! You will need to wash the knife and board after chopping too.

## HOW TO PEEL AND CRUSH GARLIC

- Put the clove of garlic on to a chopping board and chop the pointy top off.
- Place a large chef's knife flat on top of the clove then press down on the blade hard with your free hand until the garlic splits.
- The skin should come away from the flesh very easily so you can throw it away.
- You can chop garlic by hand – in a similar way to chopping an onion – but it is so much easier to put the flesh into a garlic crusher to squish it, and it doesn't make any difference to the finished dish.

## HOW TO CHOP HERBS AND NUTS

- Pick all the leaves off the stems and pile them up in the middle of a chopping board.
- Put the tip of your knife on the chopping board on the far side of your pile of leaves and place your free hand on top of the blade (it's not sharp).
- Then, keeping the tip of the knife on the board, cut down through the herbs, moving the angle of the knife a little each time so you chop all the leaves. This is called a rock chop because your knife rocks back and forward under your second hand.
- From time to time, put the knife down and pile up the leaves again and repeat this chopping action until all the leaves have been chopped.
- This is also the way to chop whole nuts – just put them on a board and rock chop across them until they are all cut into small pieces. It can be a bit trickier as the nuts roll around more than the herbs do but keeping them close together will help.

## ANOTHER WAY TO CHOP HERBS

- Pick the leaves off the stems and put them into a mug.
- Use a pair of sharp kitchen scissors to cut downwards into the mug.
- Keep cutting until the leaves are all chopped up. How easy is that?

I LOVE HERBS AND PUT THEM IN ALMOST EVERYTHING I COOK

# ESSENTIAL KIT LIST

This is a list of things that you will need to be able cook my recipes... If you look in the cupboards at home, you will probably find most of these things ready to go. You don't need all sorts of crazy, expensive equipment to produce delicious food but it will be hard without some basic things like knives, pots and pans and a wooden spoon.

**Chopping board** This is for protecting the work top when you are slicing and dicing things with a sharp knife.

**Bowls** You can't mix stuff together without having something to mix it in! It doesn't have to be a special bowl for mixing, a salad bowl will do. Smaller bowls for making dressings and dips and for beating eggs are useful – but you can always just use a cereal bowl or mug. You'll also need a heatproof bowl that fits over a small saucepan if you want to melt chocolate (although you can do that in a microwave too, see page 176).

**A large chef's knife** A larger knife is perfect for chopping nuts and herbs (see opposite).

**A small paring knife** This is the one for cutting up fruit and vegetables and carving recorders out of carrots (see page 81)!

**Scissors** Sometimes it is easier to chop things up with scissors rather than a knife, such as bacon and herbs.

**Saucepan** Big and small pans are essential for things like cooking pasta, boiling potatoes, melting chocolate, and making sauces and syrups.

**Frying pan** A frying pan is a must-have for cooking pancakes, frying chicken and sausages and browning mince – I use a large deep one for making my lasagne (see page 130).

**Baking trays** You will need a couple of baking trays for cooking all sorts of things in the oven like my calzones (see page 92), super tasty Southern Baked-not-fried Chicken (see page 60), Baked Green Fries (see page 146), Healthy Crispy Onion Rings (see page 85), biscuits and meringues.

**Colander** This is so useful for draining pasta and vegetables after cooking, and also for rinsing tins of beans.

**Weighing scales, measuring jug and measuring spoons** Most recipes call for at least one ingredient to be weighed or measured out. Using scales for dry things like flour and sugar, a measuring jug for liquids and measuring spoons for small amounts of both dry and liquid ingredients will help you do this accurately. The more precise you are, the better the recipe will turn out.

**Wooden spoon** After a good knife, this is probably the most useful item of kit in the kitchen! You will use it to stir, mix, cream, fold and swirl virtually every time you cook.

**Whisk** Mixing things with a whisk helps to introduce air into the mixture as well as getting rid of any lumps. If you don't have an electric hand whisk or stand mixer, build up your arm muscles with a balloon whisk.

**Sieve** A sieve is for straining liquids, sifting flour or removing the seeds from cooked fruit.

**Lemon squeezer** This is for squeezing lemons, obvs. It makes the job of getting the juice out of a whole lemon really easy.

**Garlic crusher** And this is for crushing garlic, funnily enough! Super useful if you don't want to cut a small garlic clove into even tinier pieces with a knife – it takes a fraction of the time and, as an added bonus, your fingers won't smell of garlic afterwards.

**Box grater** This is essential for grating things like cheese and vegetables. It has large and small holes. You can also use the smallest holes for zesting oranges, lemons and limes and grating Parmesan, ginger and even chocolate.

**Vegetable peeler** A sharp speedy peeler makes peeling carrots, potatoes and cucumbers a piece of cake. You can also use it to make lovely long ribbons of veg – like in Mum's Favourite Noodle Salad (see page 56).

**Baking paper** Lining a baking tray with this special paper will stop your biscuits or meringues sticking to the bottom. Baking paper can also be used to make parcels for cooking fish (see page 116).

**Cling film** This is really handy for covering things up while they are marinating or rising or generally just chilling out.

**Tin foil** You will need tin foil for wrapping food up before cooking it in an open fire or just when you want to put it in the oven all wrapped up.

## SPECIAL KIT LIST

If a recipe uses a piece of equipment that isn't on the Essential Kit List above, I have made a note under the ingredients list on that recipe. This equipment isn't always completely essential but it can make things a whole lot easier – like an electric whisk, stand mixer or an apple corer.

Then there are are some recipes that need specific baking tins like cake tins of a certain size, or muffin trays, which I've also added to the special kit list. You might find you already have some of these things in your kitchen but you may also have to ask your mum and dad really nicely to buy them for you, or put them on your Christmas or birthday list.

A FRYING PAN IS A MUST HAVE FOR COOKING PANCAKES

# SOME THOUGHTS ABOUT INGREDIENTS

## ANIMAL WELFARE

I love animals almost as much as I love cooking. I'm not vegetarian but I do make an effort to only eat meat that comes from animals who have led happy lives. It is obviously better for the animals but the meat is usually more delicious too. Always wash your hands after handling raw meat.

## HAPPY CHICKENS

Try to choose eggs from free-range chickens who have lived outside and enjoyed a good quality of life. By the way, all the eggs in this book are medium sized. After you've cracked your eggs, make sure to wash your hands.

## SUSTAINABLE FISHING

It's really important to buy fish from sustainable sources so you know that the method of fishing or farming isn't damaging the oceans or fish stocks around the world. Buying sustainable fish now means that we will all be able to enjoy fish for many generations to come. Always wash your hands after touching raw fish.

## TO SEASON OR NOT?

Salt is a flavour enhancer which makes food taste, well . . . tastier, when you add it to your cooking. I try not to use too much of it because it isn't good for you but I can't imagine leaving it out all together. I therefore just add a little pinch which is literally the amount that you can pinch between your thumb and first two fingers or a couple of twists of the salt mill.

## SPICE IT UP

Lots of my recipes have chilli in them because we all like chilli in my family – especially Jack who loves everything extra hot. I like a bit of warmth but if you don't, leave the chilli out or reduce the amounts until it works for you.

## ABOUT BUTTER

The butter I use in cooking is usually salted so unless the recipes says something different, use salted butter too. If you only have unsalted butter, you may need to add a little extra salt to the finished dish.

## FLOUR POWER

The recipes in this book mostly call for plain wheat flour but occasionally I use chickpea flour, which is gluten free and tastes slightly different. It is easy to buy in supermarkets but if you can't find it, you can use plain flour instead.

CLUCK!

# RISE AND SHINE

breakfasts worth getting
out of bed for!

I love weekends when we can all eat breakfast as a family. . . I'm not sure why Jack is wearing a shower cap though!

My favourite fry-up combo!

This is a smiley pancake face like the one I made for mum's birthday!

# HEAD TO PAGE 39 TO PLAN A SURPRISE BREAKFAST IN BED!

# WAKE UP!!

I get up as soon as I wake up because I am always keen to get on with the day. I don't do anything before eating breakfast, though. Mornings can be really manic and it is the one meal that we don't all sit down and eat together because we all help ourselves.

I love porridge, smoothies and granola bars on busy days because they don't take long to make and eat (well, the granola bars need to be made in advance but they keep all week and are great when for I'm dashing out the door) and they keep you going until lunch – really important for school days. Smoothies are particularly brilliant for hectic mornings too because you can add all sorts of good things like chia seeds, flax seeds, nuts, bee pollen, yoghurt and oats as well as lots of fruit and vegetables so you know you are getting some of your five a day and lots besides. Experiment with different combinations to find out what you like best.

Weekends are different because there's more time and we are more likely to all sit down to family brunch at home. I love a good old English cooked breakfast with sausages, scrambled eggs, beans and toast but I also really enjoy American-style pancakes and waffles. Those Americans know a thing or two about breakfasts!

Breakfast fuels you up for the day ahead and makes it easier to concentrate at school, and if you skip it, you won't have the energy you need to do sports and other fun stuff. A healthy brekkie is definitely the best way to start the day.

Dad likes to eat these after he's been for a run!

# SMOOTHIE BOWLS

These yummy bowls of berry goodness will keep you going all morning because of the protein-packed chia seeds, milk and nuts which all make you feel fuller for longer. They taste awesome, too.

**Serves 4**

100g natural or Greek yoghurt

300ml milk – rice, soy, oat, almond, cow's or whatever you like

200g frozen forest fruits or frozen mixed berries

2 tbsp chia seeds

1 tbsp honey

75g mixed nuts (think almonds, Brazil, cashews, hazelnuts etc.)

100g fresh blackberries

100g fresh blueberries

Bee pollen for sprinkling (optional)

**Special kit list**

Blender or smoothie maker

1. Weigh out the yoghurt, milk and frozen fruits and put them into a blender with the chia seeds and honey. Put the lid on the blender and blitz everything together for about a minute until really smooth.

2. Lay the nuts out on a chopping board and use a big knife to chop them into tiny pieces (see page 14).

3. Spoon the blended fruit mixture into 4 bowls and decorate the top with the chopped nuts, blackberries and blueberries, then sprinkle with bee pollen if you are using it.

## TILLY'S TIP:

Soak the chia seeds in 4 tablespoons of water for 5 minutes to plump them up – or soak them overnight so they are ready to go when you wake up.

# MY FAVOURITE EXERCISE RE-BOOSTER

# SUPER STRAWBERRY SMOOTHIE

Drink your breakfast! This smoothie is really filling and packed with fresh fruit and chia seeds which are really good for you. Most fruits and vegetables can be blitzed like this, so get creative in the morning.

**Serves 4–6**

2 tbsp chia seeds

400g strawberries

2 bananas

500ml apple juice

1 tbsp bee pollen or a spoonful of honey

**Special kit list**

Blender or smoothie maker

1. Put the chia seeds in a bowl and cover with 4 tablespoons of water. Leave them to soak for 5 minutes while you get everything else ready.
2. Remove the green bits from the top of the strawberries and put the fruit into the blender.
3. Peel the bananas and break them each into 4 big chunks then add them to the blender with the strawberries.
4. Pour in the apple juice and add the soaked chia seeds and the bee pollen.
5. Put the lid on the blender then blitz everything together for about a minute until nice and smooth.
6. Pour into glasses and serve.

## TILLY'S TIP:

You can also add green things to this smoothie, like spinach, kale or broccoli. Adding vegetables might sound weird but you can't really taste them and you get all those vitamins without even trying! You can also swap the apple juice for almond or oat milk or coconut water, and add milled seeds and nuts for extra protein.

**Dad says...**

When measuring things like honey or syrup, coat the measuring jug, bowl or spoon with a thin layer of vegetable or sunflower oil beforehand so all the sticky stuff gets into the mixture rather than left behind.

# GRANOLA BARS

These granola bars take a bit of time to make so don't start them 10 minutes before the school run! Make them the night before instead. They will last for up to 5 days in an airtight container.

These home-made cereal bars are really great for breakfast when you're rushing to get out of the door in a hurry – most days in my case! And because they are made with natural sweeteners, they are much better for you than shop-bought ones.

## Makes 12–14 bars

180g soft dates

360ml runny honey

60g pecans

60g dried apricots

250g rolled oats

30g sunflower seeds

120g unsweetened desiccated coconut

2 tbsp chia seeds

Vegetable or sunflower oil, for greasing the tins

## Special kit list

Blender or food processor

Brownie tin (approximately 23 x 23cm)

1. Heat your oven to 180°C/160°C fan/gas mark 4.

2. Remove and throw away the stones from the dates, then put the dates in a small saucepan with the honey. Bring to the boil then blitz in your blender until you have a smooth paste. Leave to cool a little while you get the rest of your ingredients ready.

3. Roughly chop the pecans with a large knife (see page 14), then chop the dried apricots.

4. Put the oats, pecans, apricots, sunflower seeds, coconut and chia seeds into a mixing bowl and add the date paste. Mix everything together really well.

5. Line a brownie tin (approximately 23cm square) with baking paper and brush it with a little tasteless oil like vegetable oil. Pour the granola mixture on top, pressing it into the corners and making sure it is roughly flat on top.

6. Put the tray into the oven for 40 minutes until lightly brown on top, then remove the tray from the oven and leave to cool completely.

7. Cut into bars and try not to eat them all or you won't have any left for your breakfast!

# AMERICAN PANCAKES WITH BLUEBERRIES AND BACON

These are thick pancakes like they serve stacked up with crispy bacon and maple syrup in American diners. I love them because I really like the combination of sweet, smoky and salty flavours.

**Serves 4**

30g butter

225g plain flour

1 tbsp baking powder

2 tbsp caster sugar

2 eggs

300ml whole milk

A few drizzles of vegetable or sunflower oil, to grease the pan

8 rashers of back or streaky bacon

200g blueberries

2 tbsp maple syrup

1. Put the butter into a small pan and gently melt it over a low heat. When it has melted, put the pan to one side to allow the butter to cool.

2. In the meantime, put the flour, baking powder and sugar into a mixing bowl and mix everything together.

3. Crack the eggs into a jug and beat them with a fork until the whites and yolks are mixed together. Remember to wash your hands if you get raw egg on your fingers. Add the milk and cooled butter and stir well.

4. Pour the wet ingredients into the bowl of flour, a little at a time, and use a whisk to mix them together. This should hopefully mean there aren't any lumps in your batter.

5. Place a large frying pan over a medium heat and add a drizzle of oil. Once it is hot, add the bacon rashers and fry for 3 minutes on each side or until crispy. Beware of spitting bacon fat! (If you can't fit all the bacon in the pan at the same time, cook it in two batches.)

6. While the bacon is cooking, get started making the pancakes: place a second large, non-stick, frying pan over a medium heat and once it is hot, add a drizzle of oil. Using a small ladle, pour a spoonful of batter into the pan to make a pancake about 10–12cm wide. Pour another spoonful of batter next to it to make a second pancake – try not to let them touch and become one big pancake! Cook for 2 to 3 minutes and then turn (or flip, if you're brave enough!) them over and cook for a further 2 minutes. Remove the pancakes from the pan and keep them warm under a layer of foil. Repeat this step until all the batter is used up, adding another drizzle of oil to the pan if you need to. You should end up with about 12 pancakes. Keep an eye on the bacon!

7. When the bacon is cooked, remove it from the pan and drain on some kitchen paper.

8. Place a single pancake or a little stack of them in the centre of each plate and decorate with the bacon, blueberries and maple syrup.

# TILLY'S TIP:

To make a face on your pancakes, drizzle a little batter into the hot pan in the shape of a smile for the mouth and two small circles for eyes. You could make any shapes you like but they don't take very long to cook because they are much thinner than the pancakes so be careful not to burn them. Stick blueberry eyes on with a little maple syrup.

# CHEAT'S CHOCOLATEY 'CHURROS'

This is an easy, healthier version of one of Jack's favourite street food snacks. In Spain, original home of the churro, they eat them dipped in chocolate or milky coffee for breakfast which sounds like a great way to start the day to me. They are delicious for pudding or a snack, too!

**Serves 4–6**

1 x 320g packet of ready rolled puff pastry

100g butter

2 tbsp ground cinnamon

115g granulated sugar

240g chocolate sauce

1. Heat your oven to 220°C/200°C fan/gas mark 7.
2. Line a baking tray with a piece of baking paper.
3. Cut the puff pastry into strips about 3cm wide and 10cm long, and lay them on the baking tray – leave some space between each one.
4. Put the tray into the preheated oven and bake for 15 to 20 minutes until golden brown.
5. While the 'churros' are cooking, put the butter into a small saucepan and melt it over a low heat. Remove the pan from the hob and pour the butter into a bowl.
6. Mix the cinnamon and sugar together and spread it out on a plate.
7. When the 'churros' come out of the oven, leave them to cool for a couple of minutes then dip each one in the melted butter then roll in the cinnamon sugar to finish.
8. Warm the chocolate sauce in a small saucepan over a low heat and serve it in a bowl in the middle of the table so everyone can dip their 'churros' in.

## TILLY'S TIP:

Use a pizza wheel to sail through your pastry. It is even easier than using a knife.

### Dad says...

You're a cheat, Tilly Ramsay! These aren't proper churros! . . . but I have to admit they taste really good and they're so much easier to make than the real thing.

# WAFFLES WITH FRIED EGGS AND MAPLE SYRUP

I love waffles – who doesn't?! – and they make a really scrummy weekend breakfast or brunch. You will need a waffle maker but they are not very expensive and so much fun (but see my note in the Special Kit List). You can then make waffles for breakfast, brunch, lunch and tea!

**Serves 4**

100g butter

260g plain flour or chickpea flour (or you can use half and half)

1 tbsp baking powder

425ml whole milk

3 tbsp caster sugar

Salt and pepper

3 eggs (plus 4 eggs for frying)

1 tbsp vegetable or sunflower oil

Maple syrup, for drizzling

**Special kit list**

Waffle maker (or you can use a griddle pan – cook spoonfuls of the batter in a lightly greased hot pan, then turn them over to cook the other side)

1. Put the butter into a small saucepan and let it melt gently over a low heat. Remove the pan from the heat and allow the butter to cool while you get on with the rest of the recipe.

2. Get your waffle maker heating up to high.

3. Put the flour, melted butter, baking powder, milk, sugar and a pinch of salt in a large bowl.

4. Carefully crack in the 3 eggs. Wash your hands after cracking eggs if you get any raw egg on your fingers.

**5.** Whisk to make a smooth batter.

**6.** Pour some of the batter into your hot waffle maker to fill the grid and then close the machine for 5 minutes. Once cooked, remove the waffles and place them on a wire rack to cool. Repeat this step until you have used up all the batter.

7. Heat a large non-stick frying pan over a medium heat and add the oil. When it is hot, one at a time, crack the 4 eggs into a small bowl or ramekin and pour each one carefully from the bowl into the frying pan (see my tip). Allow them to cook for 1 to 2 minutes or until the white is no longer see-through but the yolk is still runny. Take them out of the pan with a fish slice and put them on to a plate lined with kitchen paper to soak up some of the oil.

## TILLY'S TIPS:

It's easier and safer to crack your eggs into a small bowl before putting them into the hot frying pan. You also get to remove any bits of broken shell that sneaks in before cooking!

I sometimes like to cook my eggs in metal letter shapes — make sure you oil the letters really well, place them in the pan and then pour the eggs in. When they are cooked, leave them to cool a little before easing them out of the shapes with a small knife.

### Dad says...

Don't let the frying pan get too hot when you are frying eggs – you might burn the bottom before the top of the white is cooked.

8. Put the cooked waffles on to 4 plates and put the fried eggs on top. Season with a bit of salt and pepper then drizzle with the maple syrup and tuck in immediately. Mmmmmm.

BRUNCH OF CHAMPIONS!

# NOT-SO-FULL ENGLISH BREAKFAST

Dad and I did a live English breakfast cook off with James Cordon on *The Late Late Show* and it was really hectic – especially when dad put the bacon straight on to the hot plate and it caught fire! Don't do that! This is my favourite combination for a fry up.

**Serves 4**

Drizzle of vegetable or sunflower oil

12 chipolata sausages (always buy the best quality sausages you can)

1 x 400g tin of baked beans

8 eggs

Knob of butter, plus extra for spreading on toast

Salt and pepper (optional)

4 slices of bread

1. Put a large frying pan over a medium heat and add a tiny drizzle of oil. When the oil is hot, fry the sausages in the pan for about 12 minutes, turning them over with tongs from time to time so they are nice and brown all over.

2. While the sausages are cooking, open the tin of beans and pour them into a small saucepan. Put the saucepan over a low heat to gently warm the beans through, stirring occasionally.

3. Next, crack all the eggs into a bowl and beat them with a fork or whisk until well mixed. Wash your hands if you get any raw egg on your fingers.

4. Put the butter into a saucepan or non-stick frying pan and put it over a medium-low heat. When the butter has melted, pour in the beaten eggs and stir them regularly with a spatula or wooden spoon until they begin to thicken. Continue to stir, gently moving the eggs around the pan until they are almost cooked. Take the pan off the heat at this moment because they will keep on cooking from the heat of the pan, and you don't want them to be too solid. Season with salt and pepper at this point if you like.

5. Toast the bread and spread the toast with lots of butter while it is still hot.

6. At this point, your sausages should be cooked, your beans hot and your eggs ready to be put on top of the buttered toast. Cooked breakfast perfection!

## TILLY'S TIP:

You can also cook sausages in the oven but it takes a bit longer. Heat your oven to 180°C/160° fan/gas mark 4 and cook the sausages on a baking tray with a little bit of oil for about 20 to 25 minutes, turning them over at least once while they are cooking.

# PLANNING THE PERFECT SURPRISE BREAKFAST IN BED

**Be prepared.** If you are planning to make pancakes for Mother's Day, check that there are eggs in the house the night before. It sounds obvious but it's pretty tricky to make pancakes without them! The same goes for other vital ingredients.

**Get up early.** You can't surprise your mum/dad/brother/sister with a beautiful breakfast in bed if they get up before you.

**Choose the menu carefully.** Think about who you are making breakfast for – what are their favourite foods? And also consider that some foods are easier than others to eat in bed!

**Presentation is everything.** Get a big tray and make it look cool with a place mat, vase of flowers, cards etc. You could even stick a sparkler into your stack of pancakes and light it at the last minute.

**Make the food look fun.** I made a pancake face for mum's birthday and she loved it! (See page 29.) You could use pastry cutters to cut out shapes or letters from buttered toast or make heart-shaped 'churros' (see page 30) to dip in chocolate sauce.

**Think drinks.** Find out how mum or dad like their morning tea or coffee or make a glass of freshly squeezed orange juice. You will earn yourself Brownie points for the rest of the year.

**Be quiet!** Too much giggling and stomping up the stairs will wake everyone up and ruin the surprise.

Don't make too much noise or else it won't be a surprise!

JACK, WHAT IS THAT ON YOUR HEAD!?

SURPRISE!!

# HEALTHY APPETITE

super tasty recipes that
happen to be really
good for you

Swimming pier-to-pier with Jack in California was one of the hardest things I've ever done. Finishing was such an amazing feeling!

# PADDLE BOARDING IS FAB!

Mmm! Healthy 'fried' chicken!

I love how colourful these salads are and they're really fun served in a jar!

# HEAD TO PAGE 68 FOR SOME TIPS ON EATING THE RIGHT FOOD FOR SPORT AND TRAINING

Two of my favourite things in life are sport and cooking. In fact, the whole of my family are sport and action mad. We love fitting as many adventures and new experiences as we can into every day. We're also all super competitive so if there's a possibility of beating each other, we give it everything we've got – even if it's just a water fight in the back garden! Mum and dad both do triathlons and run marathons and I play netball, hockey, water polo, rounders and do athletics and we're all crazy about swimming.

Living life to the max takes a lot of energy so, unsurprisingly, we Ramsays have very healthy appetites. Thanks to mum we eat really well most of the time, filling up with lean protein, lots of veggies, whole grains, nuts and fruit. Obviously we all like breaking the rules too (my favourite guilty snack is pickled onion-flavoured crisps! Shhhhhh), but she encourages us to mostly fuel up on the good stuff which helps when it comes to training and doing sports, not forgetting the strenuous work of growing up.

Mum's clever trick is to make food that looks and tastes awesome. If you do this, everyone will want to tuck in without even realising that what they are eating is good for them. Try some of the recipes in this chapter and you'll totally forget that this is supposed to be 'healthy food'. My bright, crunchy salads and dips look brilliant and taste equally great. They're not hard to make, either. I also like giving unhealthy classics a Tilly makeover, so you can still have delicious crispy chicken but my baked version isn't nearly as bad for you (give my baked onion rings and courgette fries on pages 85 and 146 a try, too). And as they are healthier it means you can go back for seconds!

Fish parcels are a really easy and healthy way of cooking fish – and there's not much washing up either!

SHHHH!

# RAINBOW VEG AND SPICED BEAN DIP

Mum's a total green goddess and this butter bean hummus is one of her favourite healthy snacks. It's fantastic for sharing – you just choose whatever crunchy veg you like and dip it in.

## Serves 8

2 small carrots

1/2 cucumber

4 celery sticks

1/2 head of broccoli

1 small jicama (see my tip) (optional)

1 chicory

75g sugar snap peas

1 x 400g tin of butter beans

1 garlic clove

1 lemon

Salt and pepper

1/2 tsp ground cumin

1 tbsp tahini

4 tbsp olive oil, plus extra for drizzling on the top

## Special kit list

Blender or food processor

1. Start by prepping the vegetables: peel the carrots and then cut them into sticks. Cut the cucumber and celery into similar sized sticks. Break or cut the broccoli into florets – not too small because you need to be able to hold on to the stalks when you use them for dipping. Peel and slice the jicama, if using. Chop the bottom off the chicory and pull apart the leaves – these make perfect dipping spoons! Leave the sugar snaps whole.

2. Open the tin of butter beans and pour the beans into a colander to drain away the liquid.

3. Peel the garlic clove and crush it to a paste in a garlic crusher.

4. Cut the lemon in half and squeeze out all the juice.

5. Put the butter beans, crushed garlic, lemon juice, salt and pepper, ground cumin and tahini into your blender. Turn it on and while it is blending pour in the olive oil. Blitz until smooth.

6. Put the dip into a bowl (or lidded box if you're packing it into a picnic basket) and drizzle the top with olive oil before serving with the crunchy veg.

## TILLY'S TIP:

Jicama is one of my favourite vegetables in the States – it's a bit like a Mexican turnip. It's so crunchy and delicious but if you can't find it, use tart apples, daikon radish or water chestnuts.

**CRUNCH!**

### Dad says...

To make sure your chopping board doesn't slip put a few sheets of damp kitchen roll underneath it – it won't budge whatever you are chopping or slicing, which makes it much safer.

# QUINOA CHICKEN SALAD WRAPS

The great thing about wrapping everything up in a tortilla is that it's really easy to eat wherever you go – great for picnics and packed lunches. This one is full of good things like quinoa (a magical superfood a bit like cous cous), chicken, hummus, avocado and crunchy veg.

**Serves 4**

500ml vegetable stock or water

170g quinoa

Salt and pepper

2 skinless chicken breasts

Drizzle of vegetable or sunflower oil

1 red or yellow pepper

1/4 cucumber

10 sundried tomatoes

2 avocados

Small bunch of flat-leaf parsley

1 tbsp olive oil

4 tortilla wraps (plain, multiseed, wholewheat or any flavour you like)

150g hummus

Handful of baby spinach leaves

1. Put the vegetable stock or water into a medium saucepan and place the pan over a medium heat. When it starts boiling, add the quinoa and cook for 10 minutes then take the pan off the hob. Drain the quinoa and put it into a bowl to cool. Season with a little salt and pepper.

2. While the quinoa is cooling, cut the chicken into strips. Don't forget to wash your hands afterwards.

3. Place a frying pan over a medium-high heat. When the pan is hot, drizzle in a little oil and then add the chicken.

4. Cook for 5 minutes before turning the chicken over with a pair of tongs and cooking on the other side for another 5 minutes. To test whether your chicken is cooked, see what dad says, opposite.

5. When the chicken is cooked, remove it from the pan and let it rest while you prep the veg.

6. Pull out the middle bit of the pepper where all the seeds are and throw it away, then cut the pepper into thin strips. Slice the cucumber into thickish batons. Chop the sundried tomatoes into halves or quarters.

7. Peel the avocados and slice them (see my tip on page 64) and chop the parsley (see page 14).

8. Add the rested chicken, cucumber, pepper strips, sundried tomatoes and parsley to the bowl of quinoa and give it a good mix. Drizzle over the olive oil and mix again.

9. Lay out the tortillas and spread a tablespoon of hummus on each one. Divide the quinoa mixture and spinach between each wrap and top with the avocado slices.

10. Roll over the tortillas to seal them. Slice each wrap in half diagonally and eat straight away or wrap in baking paper or foil to keep fresh for later.

**Dad says...**

If you are cooking chicken in the oven, pierce the thickest part with a sharp knife and look at the colour of the juices that run out. If the juices are clear, the chicken is cooked, but if they are pink, put it back in the oven for 5 more minutes. If you are pan-frying or grilling chicken, cut into it and have a look – if it is cooked, there should be no pink in the middle.

# VEGGIE DOGS

We all love hot dogs in my family but they are pretty unhealthy so I came up with a yummy vegetarian version that looks almost the same and tastes equally good.

The sausages need to firm up in the fridge for an hour before cooking.

**Serves 6**

200g cooked kidney beans, drained weight

2 carrots

1 tbsp coriander leaves

2 tbsp mint leaves

1/2 lime

200g fresh breadcrumbs

1/2 tsp turmeric

Salt and pepper

1 egg

60g white sesame seeds

1 tbsp vegetable or sunflower oil

6 wholewheat hot dog rolls (or regular ones)

Ketchup, mustard and mayo

**For the crunchy salad**

1 Little Gem lettuce

1/4 red cabbage

1 carrot

1/2 cucumber

1 tomato

1. Put the kidney beans into a colander and give them a rinse under the cold tap.

2. Peel the carrots and grate them, being careful not to grate your knuckles at the same time.

3. Chop the herbs (see page 14) then squeeze the juice from the lime half into a bowl.

**4.** Put the kidney beans into a large mixing bowl and mash them with a potato masher or fork until they are all broken up and mixed together.

**5.** Add the grated carrots, lime juice, breadcrumbs, turmeric and salt and pepper. Crack in the egg and add the chopped herbs. Mix together with clean hands, until everything is evenly mixed through.

**6.** Spread out the sesame seeds in a shallow bowl or on a plate.

**7.** Shape the mixture into 6 hot dog-style sausages. Coat them lightly in oil, using your fingers, then roll in the sesame seeds to cover them all over. Put the sausages in the fridge for about an hour to firm up.

### Dad says...

If you wet your hands before you shape the mix into sausages, it will be much easier because the mixture won't stick to your hands as much. This is also true when you are making meatballs or burgers.

8. Heat your oven to 200°C/180°C fan/gas mark 6 and line a baking tray with some foil.

9. Put the chilled sausages on to the foil-lined baking tray and bake in the hot oven for 10 to 15 minutes until the sesame seeds are toasted and the sausages are heated through.

10. While your hot dogs are cooking, prep your crunchy salad. Shred the lettuce and red cabbage. Peel the carrot and chop into thin sticks. Chop the cucumber into thin sticks too. Cut the tomato in half and scoop out the seeds. Chop the flesh into thin slices and mix the carrot, cucumber and tomato with the leaves.

11. Cut open the rolls and spread with some ketchup, mustard and mayo in whatever combination you like then put the veggie hot dogs inside and top with more ketchup, mustard and mayo and crunchy salad.

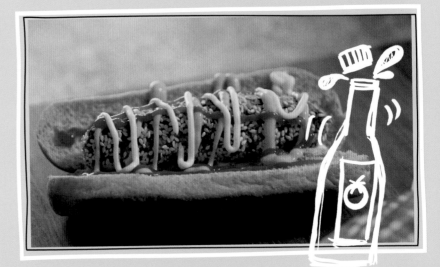

## Dad says...

Thigh meat is the most tender part of the chicken and brilliant for grilling or barbecuing because it doesn't dry out as easily as the breast. If you can't buy boneless thigh meat, either ask your butcher to de-bone 4 thighs for you or learn how to do it yourself! It isn't hard and is a really handy skill to have.

# LEAN MACHINE CHICKEN SKEWERS

The chicken needs to sit in the marinade for at least an hour before cooking.

We eat a lot of chicken in our house and I love finding new and tasty ways to serve it. This combination of pine nuts, Parmesan and sun-blushed tomatoes is amazing and so moreish . . .

## Serves 4

50g pine nuts

1 garlic clove

1 red chilli (optional)

50g Parmesan cheese

200g sun-blushed tomatoes in oil (you may also need some extra olive oil)

500g chicken (preferably thigh – see what dad says, opposite)

2 tbsp flat-leaf parsley leaves

## Special kit list

Blender or food processor

Skewers (if they are wooden, soak them for 20 minutes in water before using so they won't burn or catch fire under the grill!)

## TILLY'S TIP:

These are scrummy cooked on a barbecue too. Make sure they are put on to the grill when it's at its hottest so you can be sure that the chicken is cooked all the way through.

1. First, toast the pine nuts: place a frying pan over a medium heat and put the pine nuts into the pan for about 5 minutes, moving them around often so they don't burn. Tip them on to a small plate.

2. Peel the garlic clove and crush it to a paste in a garlic crusher.

3. Remove the seeds from the red chilli, if using, and dice into small pieces (see page 13).

4. Grate the Parmesan cheese, using the fine side of the grater, and being careful not to grate your fingers!

5. Drain the sun-blushed tomatoes over a measuring jug so you catch all the yummy oil. Have a look how much oil you have – you need 175ml so if you have less than this, top up with olive oil.

6. Put the crushed garlic, toasted pine nuts, sun-blushed tomatoes, chilli (if you are adding it), Parmesan cheese and oil into your blender and, with the lid on, blitz to a loose paste. Put the paste into a large mixing bowl.

7. Chop the chicken into chunks. Add them to the bowl and mix thoroughly, then put the chicken into the fridge for at least 1 hour. Always wash your hands when you have been touching raw meat.

8. Once the chicken has had a chance to marinate, preheat the grill to high.

9. Thread the chicken on to the skewers and put them on to a grill tray.

10. Cook under the grill for 5 minutes and then turn them over and grill again on the other side for the same amount of time. Make sure the chicken is properly cooked all the way through (see what dad says on page 47 for how to do this).

11. While the chicken is cooking, chop the parsley with a large knife or put the leaves into a cup and chop them with scissors (see page 14).

12. Transfer the cooked chicken skewers to a serving plate and garnish with the chopped parsley. Nailed it.

# SUPER SALMON PARCELS

**Dad says...**
When you are squeezing the juice out of the lemon halves, hold them with the cut side up – the juice will still run down into the dish but the pips will stay in the lemon.

Wrapping fish and vegetables up in paper like this is so easy, plus, none of the fantastic flavours can escape while they are cooking – it's very clever. You can also serve up the salmon in their parcels, like a present! Just warn everyone to be careful, as hot steam will come out when they open them.

## Serves 4

1 courgette

1 small leek

1 red pepper

1 lemon

Small handful of chives

1 tbsp tarragon leaves

1 tbsp flat-leaf parsley leaves

4 salmon fillets (approx. 150g each), with or without skin

Salt and pepper

2 tbsp olive oil

## Special kit list

4 pieces of baking paper (approximately 20 x 30cm)

1. Heat your oven to 220°C/200°C fan/gas mark 7.

2. While the oven is heating up, finely slice the courgette, leek and red pepper into strips (throwing away the seeded bit inside the pepper). Cut the lemon in half and cut one half into slices.

3. Chop the herbs (see page 14) until they are very small then mix them together.

4. Cut out 4 pieces of baking paper about 20 x 30cm. Pile up strips of veg in the middle of each piece and top with a fish fillet. Arrange some more veg around the fish and a few pieces on top. Season with a little salt and pepper. Remember to wash your hands after handling raw fish.

5. Drizzle each fillet with half a tablespoon of olive oil and a squeeze of lemon juice from the unsliced half (see what day says). Top with the lemon slices and herbs.

6. Fold the paper over the fish so that the ends meet. Fold the edges over a couple of times but don't wrap the fish too tight – the parcel needs to be able to puff up a bit during the cooking. Then fold in both ends and staple them closed so no juice or flavour can escape.

7. Put the parcels on to a baking tray and cook in the oven for 15 minutes until the fish and vegetables are cooked. To check whether the fish is cooked, carefully open one of the parcels to see whether the fish is opaque and flakes easily when pressed gently with a fork. If this isn't the case, the fillets might need a bit more cooking.

8. Carefully remove the salmon fillets and vegetables from the parcels and put them on to 4 plates. Drizzle the juices from the baking paper over the fish before you serve them.

# MUM'S FAVOURITE NOODLE SALAD

Mum loves this super healthy salad – it's crunchy, colourful, sweet, hot and sharp all at the same time. There is quite a lot of chopping (good for practising your knife skills) but once that's done you just mix it all together.

> **Dad says...**
> Use the tip of a teaspoon to peel the skin off the ginger. It makes it really easy to get into all the nooks and crannies and you don't lose any of the flesh as you go.

## Serves 6

1 x 250g packet of Japanese rice noodles or vermicelli

3 cooked chicken breasts, skin removed

6 spring onions

1/2 cucumber

1 red pepper

1 medium carrot

2 tbsp coriander leaves

2 tbsp roasted unsalted peanuts

2 tbsp roasted unsalted cashews

1 tbsp sesame seeds

250g cooked peeled prawns

125g bean sprouts

### For the dressing

A thumb-sized piece of fresh ginger

3 tbsp reduced salt soy sauce

1 tsp Sriracha hot sauce or sweet chilli sauce

4 tbsp sesame oil

2 tbsp rice vinegar

2 tsp runny honey

1. Follow the packet instructions for cooking the noodles. When they are ready, drain them in a colander and run them under the cold tap for a little while to stop them cooking. Leave them to cool completely.

2. While the noodles are cooling, prepare the other ingredients. Shred the chicken breasts by pulling the meat apart with two forks.

3. Slice the spring onions into rings. Cut the cucumber in half lengthways, scrape out the seeds and slice each half.

4. Chop the pepper in half and pull out the middle bit where all the seeds are and throw it away. Slice each half into fine strips.

5. Peel the carrot and use the peeler to slice it into long ribbons.

6. To make the dressing, peel the piece of ginger and grate it on the fine side of your grater, being careful not to grate your fingers at the same time!

7. Measure out all the other dressing ingredients and put them into a mixing bowl with the ginger then stir everything together. Dressing sorted.

8. Chop the coriander leaves with a large knife or in a mug with a pair of scissors (see page 14). Then chop the nuts together until they are in small pieces (see page 14).

9. To toast the sesame seeds, put them into a frying pan over a medium heat without any oil. Let them cook for about 3 to 5 minutes, stirring them often with a wooden spoon so they don't burn. Then tip them onto a small plate.

10. Put the noodles into a large salad bowl and add the shredded chicken, prawns, bean sprouts, chopped up vegetables and coriander.

11. Mix everything together then pour over the dressing and give it a stir so everything is lightly coated.

12. Spoon the noodle salad into serving bowls and sprinkle with the chopped nuts and sesame seeds. So tasty . . .

### Dad says...

If you grate vegetables over a plate rather than on to a chopping board, it is really easy to move all the grated veg/fruit to the pan, wok or bowl rather than spending ages trying to get all the little bits off the chopping board. You know it makes sense . . .

CRUNCH!

# HOLLYWOOD HILLS CRUNCH

This coleslaw is super healthy, super delicious and super Californian! It's so simple to make as there's no cooking involved – just shred the leaves and mix up the dressing. You can hear the crunch all the way from Hollywood . . . It goes brilliantly with grilled chicken or steak and would be great at a barbecue.

**Serves 4**

1 head of Chinese leaf (about 150g)

1 bunch of curly kale

2 large carrots

1 1/2 tbsp flat-leaf parsley leaves

1 1/2 tbsp coriander leaves

**For the dressing**

1 small red or green apple

150g Greek yoghurt

1 tbsp runny honey

1/2 tbsp cider vinegar

Salt and pepper

1. Peel off the leaves from the Chinese leaf. Keep a few to one side for serving, then shred the rest with a large knife.

2. Pull the kale leaves off the tough stems then rip the leaves into smaller pieces.

3. Peel the carrots then grate them, being careful not to grate your knuckles in the process!

4. Roughly chop the parsley and coriander leaves with a large knife or in a mug with a pair of scissors (see page 14).

5. Put all of the vegetables and herbs into a salad bowl, then make the dressing. Start by grating the apple (with the skin still on). Again, watch out for your knuckles!

6. Put the grated apple into a small bowl with the yoghurt, honey and vinegar, season with salt and pepper and mix everything together. If it's a bit thick, loosen it with some water.

7. Just before serving, cover the leaves with the dressing and mix together well. I like to serve the salad with a few whole Chinese leaves around the edge of the plate.

## TILLY'S TIPS:

Putting the dressing on the salad at the last minute helps to keep the crunch factor. No one wants soggy salad. . .

Try to get your hands on bunches of kale, rather than kale that is already chopped up. You won't have so many stalks.

# SOUTHERN BAKED-NOT-FRIED CHICKEN

This is my healthy take on an American favourite – fried chicken – which is usually, funnily enough, fried. I coat it in My Top Secret Spice Mix then bake it in the oven which makes it much better for you but it's just as tasty. It's really nice with Baked Green Fries (see page 146) and salad or the Super Tomato Mess on page 155.

## TILLY'S TIP:

Try using different combinations of flours – half chickpea flour and half regular wheat flour works well. Regular porridge oats blitzed in a blender is also a great crunchy alternative.

**Serves 4**

60g ground almonds

60g oat flour

60g chickpea flour

2 tsp onion powder or granules

1 tsp smoked paprika

1 tsp celery salt

1 tsp garlic powder

3 eggs

4 boneless chicken thighs and 4 chicken drumsticks (or 8 boneless chicken thighs)

Olive oil, to drizzle

1. Heat your oven to 180°C/160°C fan/gas mark 4. Line a baking tray with foil or baking paper.

2. Put the ground almonds, oat flour, chickpea flour, onion powder, smoked paprika, celery salt and garlic powder into a mixing bowl and mix everything together.

**3.** Crack the eggs into a small bowl and beat with a fork or whisk until well mixed. Remember to wash your hands if you get any raw egg on your fingers.

**4.** Dip the chicken thighs and legs in the beaten egg followed by the seasoned flour, making sure the chicken is well coated (see my tip over the page). Put them on to the lined tray. Wash your hands well after handling raw meat. Drizzle the coated chicken pieces with a little olive oil.

**5.** Put the tray into the oven for 30 to 40 minutes or until the chicken is golden brown and cooked all the way through (see dad's advice on page 47 on how to check that your chicken is cooked).

## TILLY'S TIP:

When you're coating the chicken in the eggs and flour, use one hand for dipping and coating and keep one hand clean so you can turn on the tap to wash your hands!

# I LOVE GETTING MESSY IN THE KITCHEN!

Try this super tasty, healthy version of fried chicken with my favourite Baked Green Fries (see page 146) and Super Tomato Mess (see page 155).

# CAPTAIN TILLY'S SUPER SECRET COATING!

# SHAKE AND GO RAINBOW SALAD

Food should taste good but I like it to look good too. This salad is so bright and I think it looks brilliant when you serve it in individual jars so you can see all the coloured stripes before you shake it.

## Serves 4

4 rashers of bacon (or you can use pre-cooked crispy bacon pieces)

2 hard-boiled eggs, peeled

1 romaine lettuce

20 cherry tomatoes

1 avocado

1/2 lemon

1 x 320g tin of sweetcorn, drained

## For the dressing

2 tbsp red wine vinegar

1 tbsp lemon juice

1 tsp Dijon mustard

Salt and pepper

3 tbsp olive oil

## Special kit list

4 clean 500ml preserving jars

### Dad says...

There is no need to add oil to the pan when frying bacon like this as the fat from the bacon melts down and cooks the meat.

1. Chop the bacon into small pieces using a knife or scissors. Remember to wash your hands after handling raw meat.

2. Put a frying pan over a medium heat and add the bacon pieces. Fry for about 5 minutes until the bacon is nicely crisp. Put the cooked bacon on to a plate lined with kitchen paper to drain away the fat and leave to cool.

3. While the bacon is cooling, chop the hard-boiled eggs and shred the lettuce with a large knife. Cut the cherry tomatoes in half.

4. Chop the avocado (see my tip) and squeeze the lemon over the top.

5. Put the ingredients into the jars in layers – maybe start with sweetcorn then add the tomatoes, chopped egg, bacon, avocado and finally the lettuce.

6. To make the dressing, whisk together the red wine vinegar, lemon juice and Dijon mustard in a small bowl. Season with salt and pepper, then drizzle in the olive oil, whisking continuously until it thickens.

7. When ready to eat (but not before), divide the dressing between the 4 jars and put the lids on tightly before giving them to your guests. Get them to give the jars a good shake to mix everything up before pouring the salad out on to their plates and tucking in.

## TILLY'S TIP:

Use a spoon to get the avocado out of its skin. It comes away really easily and leaves no avocado behind. Slice the avocado in half around the stone and then twist to split it in two. Remove the stone (it should come out easily if the avocado is ripe) then carefully edge the tip of the spoon in between the flesh and the skin at one end. Keep pushing the spoon — with its back against the skin — and scoop out the flesh all the way round, ready for slicing or chopping.

IF YOU DON'T HAVE JARS, JUST
MIX EVERYTHING TOGETHER IN
A BIG SALAD BOWL

# ENERGY BALLS

These power-packed energy balls have vitamins A, B, C, D and E in them: vitamin A is from the apricots, B is from the avocado, C is from the cherries, D is from the plain yoghurt and E is from the almonds. They happen to be really tasty, too . . .

**Makes 8–12 balls**

20g dark chocolate

10 dried apricots

¼ avocado

40g dried sour cherries

1 tbsp natural yoghurt

40g almonds

10 dates (without stones!)

½ tbsp runny honey

2 tsp vanilla bean paste (optional)

Handful of ground almonds, if needed

125g desiccated coconut

**Special kit list**

Food processor

1. Grate the dark chocolate using the fine side of your grater, being careful not to grate your fingers at the same time.
2. Put the apricots, avocado flesh, cherries, natural yoghurt, almonds, dates, honey and vanilla (if using) into the food processor. Add the grated chocolate and blend until the mixture comes together. (If your mix is a little too wet, add a handful of ground almonds and blend again.)
3. Carefully remove the blade from the food processor, and then, with clean hands, roll the mix into 8 to 12 balls and put them on to a clean plate or tray.
4. Spread the coconut on to a large plate and roll each ball in the coconut.
5. Keep the balls in the fridge until you are ready to eat them as this will firm them up.

These energy balls are really easy to make and don't even need any cooking. I keep some in the fridge for when I need a quick boost of energy. Power up!

# HOW TO FUEL UP FOR SPORTS AND TRAINING

I love sport and everyone in my family is always training for something so we're always trying to eat well before matches, races or competitions. Here's my guide to filling up on the right things to help you do your best when it matters.

## WHAT TO EAT WHEN

**The night before.** It's super important that your body has plenty of energy when it needs it and the best source of instantly accessible energy is carbohydrate. Load up on carbs the night before a match or race and you will have put some energy in the bank. Good carbs for the night before are jacket potatoes, pasta, bread, rice, sweet potatoes, bananas and raisins.

**The morning of.** Eating a really good breakfast on a match or training day is another good way of filling up your energy tank. Again, choose carbs like porridge, toast, cereal, bagels, waffles, bananas and fruit with a bit of protein too – think milk with your cereal, peanut butter on your bagel or a poached egg on your waffles.

**An hour before.** A carb-based snack is a good idea for a last-minute energy boost but don't eat for at least 30 minutes before starting exercise so your body has time to digest. Good pre-match snacks include nuts, seeds and dried fruit, rice

cakes spread with nut butter, energy balls (see page 67) or my personal favourite, home-made granola bars (see page 27).

**Afterwards.** You should always eat something after a big race or match and the focus should be on protein to help your muscles repair themselves. Protein is found in things like meat, cheese, yoghurt, nuts and seeds but one of the easiest ways to eat it is in a smoothie made with nuts and seeds, and milk or yoghurt. After the pier-to-pier race in L.A., Jack and I immediately tucked into my Smoothie Bowls (see page 22) and they were just what we both needed.

Jack and I enjoying our smoothies after the pier-to-pier race.

## REMEMBER TO DRINK

Dehydration has a major effect on how you perform. Carry a water bottle with you and drink little and often to keep topped up.

## THINGS TO AVOID

⦿ So-called energy drinks contain lots of sugar that causes your blood sugar levels to spike, leaving you tired when the rush wears off.

⦿ Caffeinated drinks have a similar effect but will also make you need the loo more often and dehydrate you in the long run.

⦿ Sugary snack bars and milk chocolate will play havoc with your sugar levels.

⦿ At the opposite end of the scale, don't eat too much fibre (like beans) before a match as it is difficult to digest and might leave you feeling sluggish.

GO TEAM!!

# SHARING IS CARING

everything tastes better when
you cook for your friends

I love cooking for my friends and family and having fun in the kitchen — after all, sharing really is caring!

A healthy take on onion rings.

Super cooling Californian Cooler.

Hanging out with Katy Perry and Britney Spears!

Though I do sometimes cook for just me, making food for other people is what makes me really happy. My friends are pretty keen on my cooking, too! They love coming round for home-made pizza or cakes and they're always really impressed, even when the recipe is super simple. That's the great thing about cooking – you only need to make a little bit of effort and everyone loves it!

Our house is always full of people as we four kids always have lots of friends coming and going. Meals with friends are really laid back and I love making the sort of dishes that you put into the middle of the table so everyone can tuck in and help themselves. Things like chicken skewers, sticky ribs, dips and nachos. It's a fun and sociable way to eat and you can eat everything with your fingers, which saves on the washing up!

It's the sort of food that is perfect for when friends come over for movie nights and sleepovers. It's not difficult to cook but easy to share without making masses of mess (though you will definitely need a bunch of napkins after eating those sticky ribs!). And your mum will be delighted that you've done the cooking for your friends . . . she might be even be more inclined to let people come over next time. Result!

It can also be fun getting people to help with the cooking. My friends love it, especially now they realise that I'm not bossy in the kitchen like dad! Or, get them to cook some food at home and bring it with them so you make a dish each and tuck into each other's food. Sharing is caring, after all.

HEAD TO PAGE 98 FOR SOME TIPS ON TAKING GREAT PHOTOS FOR YOUR BLOG

My totally delicious Chicken Tikka Skewers we had at our Bollywood party!

# L.A. NACHOS

These are super quick and easy to make (especially if you buy a pot of salsa rather than make it yourself) and everyone loves them. Just put them in the middle of the table and watch them disappear . . .

*If you buy the salsa rather than make it from scratch.*

**Serves 8**

1 large cooked chicken breast

200g Cheddar cheese

1 x 400g tin of kidney beans

200g lightly salted tortilla chips

125g sliced jalapeños from a jar (optional)

2 avocados

2 tbsp coriander leaves

150g sour cream

**For the salsa**

4 large tomatoes

1 large red chilli (optional)

1 small red onion

1 tbsp coriander leaves

1 lime

Salt

## TILLY'S TIP:

If some of your family and friends love jalapeños and some don't, put them at one end of the dish but not in the other end, that way everyone is happy — just remember which end is which!

**To make the salsa**

1. Chop the tomatoes into quarters and remove the seeds with a teaspoon. Finely chop the flesh and put it into a mixing bowl.

2. Remove the seeds from the red chilli, if using, and finely dice (see page 13).

3. Peel the onion and chop it to a fine dice (see page 13).

4. Chop the coriander with a large knife or in a mug with a pair of scissors (see page 14). Cut the lime in half and squeeze out the juice.

5. Add the chopped chilli, onion, coriander and lime juice to the tomatoes, then season with a pinch of salt and mix together well.

**To make the nachos**

1. Heat your oven to 200°C/180°C fan/gas mark 6.

2. While the oven is heating up, use 2 forks to pull the chicken breast apart until it is all shredded.

3. Grate the Cheddar cheese, being careful not to grate your fingers!

4. Drain and rinse the kidney beans in a colander.

5. Cover the bottom of an oven-proof dish or roasting tin, roughly 35 x 22cm, with tortilla chips and sprinkle with half the Cheddar cheese followed by the kidney beans and then the shredded chicken. Dot with the sliced jalapeño chillies if you are using them, then cover with the rest of the cheese.

6. Cook in the oven for 10 to 15 minutes or until the cheese has melted and turned bubbly and golden brown.

7. While the nachos are cooking, cut the avocados in half and remove the stones. Remove the flesh from the peel and cut into slices (see my tip on page 64).

8. Roughly chop the coriander leaves with a large knife or in a mug with a pair of scissors (see page 14).

9. Place the cooked nachos in the centre of the table and lay the avocado slices on top then put spoonfuls of the salsa and sour cream on top. Sprinkle with the coriander and get everyone to tuck in.

# TORTILLA CUPS

These crunchy tortilla cups are like a mini hand-held meal so you can eat them in front of a film or with friends at a sleepover. You can take them with you on a picnic too – I made these for our incredible day at the go-kart track in L.A. and they went down a storm.

**Makes 12**

12 rashers of streaky bacon

6 large soft tortilla wraps

150g Cheddar cheese

A little vegetable or sunflower oil, for greasing

8 eggs

Salt and pepper

6 spring onions

150g cherry tomatoes

2 tbsp chopped chives

**Special kit list**

One 12-hole muffin tin or two 6-hole muffin tins

1. Heat your oven to 180°C/160°C fan/gas mark 4.

2. While the oven is heating up, chop the bacon into small pieces. You can use a knife for this but scissors are even easier. Always wash your hands after handling raw meat.

3. Put a large frying pan over a medium heat and add the bacon pieces. Fry for about 5 minutes until the bacon is nicely cooked and smelling really tasty. (See what dad says on page 64 about why you don't need to add any oil.)

4. Put the bacon on to a plate lined with kitchen paper to drain away the fat and leave to cool.

5. In the meantime, cut each of the tortilla wraps into eight even triangles.

6. Grate the Cheddar cheese, being careful not to grate your fingers!

**7.** Grease the muffin tin (or tins) with a little oil, then line each muffin hole with the tortilla triangles – 4 in each – making sure they are overlapping. Trim them to fit so the base isn't too thick, but make sure there are no gaps, otherwise the mixture will leak out.

**8.** Crack the eggs into a large jug, season with a little salt and pepper and whisk until well mixed. Remember to wash your hands if you get any raw egg on your fingers.

**9.** Finely slice the spring onions and cut the cherry tomatoes into quarters.

**10.** Divide the spring onions, cherry tomato quarters and cooled bacon between the 12 tortilla cups, putting some of each ingredient in each one.

**11.** Pour the egg into the cups, being careful not to fill them right to the top as the mixture may spill out as it cooks. Sprinkle with some of the chopped chives (keep back some as a garnish) and top with the grated Cheddar cheese.

**12.** Cook in the oven for 20 to 25 minutes or until the cheese has melted and turned golden brown.

**13.** Allow the cups to cool a bit then remove them from the muffin tin. Just before serving, sprinkle them with the rest of the chopped chives.

## TILLY'S TIP:

These tortilla cups are really easy to adapt, depending on what you have in your fridge. If you don't have bacon, you can use chopped up ham instead. Sliced olives, cooked chopped peppers, mushrooms and spinach are also really tasty — just don't try and pack too much in or else they won't hold together.

**TILLY'S TIP:**

To make the carrots into instruments, cut the tops and bottoms off them (no need to peel them, just give them a good wash) and use an apple corer, sharp knife or thick skewer (depending on the thickness of the carrots) to hollow them out. Then use a sharp knife to carve holes and a mouthpiece in one side so they look like recorders.

# CARROT INSTRUMENTS WITH KALE AND ARTICHOKE DIP

If you just cut the carrots into sticks!

For our poptastic day in L.A. when Megan went to see Britney Spears in concert, I made musical instruments out of carrots which we dipped in to this scrummy mix of kale, artichokes, yoghurt and lemon.

I stuck a musical mouthpiece into my carrot so it could make an even louder noise!

**Serves 4**

8 large carrots

1 bunch of kale or cavolo nero

1 shallot

1 garlic clove

1 tbsp olive oil

Salt and pepper

1 lemon

100g marinated artichokes from a jar

500g Greek yoghurt

1 tbsp wholegrain mustard (optional)

1. Give the carrots a good wash and carve them into recorder or flute shapes, making holes and a mouthpiece (see my tip). Alternatively, peel the carrots and cut them in half across the middle then chop the halves into about 6 sticks each.

2. Cut out the central stalks from each of the kale or cavolo nero leaves and slice the leaves finely.

3. Peel the shallot and finely dice – think of it like a mini onion (see page 13).

4. Peel the garlic clove and crush it in a garlic crusher.

5. Heat the olive oil in a large frying pan over a medium heat and add the shredded kale or cavolo nero. Cook for a few minutes until it begins to wilt.

6. Add the chopped shallot and crushed garlic and cook for another minute. Season with salt and pepper, remove the pan from the heat and leave to cool.

7. While the kale or cavolo nero is cooling, carefully zest the lemon using the small holes on a box grater, then cut the lemon in half. Squeeze the juice from one of the halves (save the other half for another recipe).

8. Drain the artichokes from the jar and roughly chop them.

9. In a large mixing bowl, mix together the yoghurt, lemon juice, lemon zest, artichokes, wholegrain mustard (if using) and cooked kale or cavolo nero mixture. Serve with the carrot sticks or instruments for dipping.

# CHICKEN TIKKA SKEWERS

The chicken needs to marinate for 30 minutes to an hour.

We made these chicken skewers for our Bollywood party in L.A. and everyone in my family has loved them ever since. They're brilliant for sharing, served with cucumber raita or mango chutney.

**Serves 4–6**

2cm piece of fresh ginger

2 garlic cloves

3 spring onions

1 lime

1 tbsp coriander leaves

2 tsp ground cumin

2 tsp ground coriander

Pinch of chilli powder (optional)

2 tbsp tomato purée

300g natural yoghurt

200ml coconut milk

950g chicken (chicken breast or thighs or a combination – see what dad says on page 52)

2 red, yellow or orange peppers

**Special kit list**

6 skewers (if they are wooden, soak them for 20 minutes in water before using so they don't burn)

1. First make your marinade: peel the ginger with a teaspoon and grate it using the fine side of the grater, and being careful not to grate your fingers too, then put it into a large mixing bowl.

2. Peel the garlic cloves and crush in a garlic crusher. Add the garlic to the ginger in the bowl.

3. Slice the spring onions finely and throw them in the bowl too.

4. Cut the lime in half and squeeze the juice into the mixing bowl.

5. Chop the coriander leaves with a big knife or in a mug with a pair of scissors (see page 14) and put it in the bowl.

6. Measure out the cumin, ground coriander, chilli if using, tomato purée, yoghurt and coconut milk, then put them all into the bowl and mix everything together.

7. Chop the chicken into chunks. Add them to the marinade and leave to marinate in the fridge for 30 minutes to an hour.

8. Heat your oven to 200°C/180°C fan/gas mark 6.

9. While the oven is heating up, cut the tops off the peppers, remove and throw away the seeds, then chop the peppers into 2cm pieces.

10. With clean hands, thread the chicken and peppers on to the soaked wooden skewers or metal skewers – I like 2 pieces of chicken and then 1 piece of pepper and then repeat – and put them on to a baking tray. Always wash your hands when you have touched raw meat.

11. Put the tray into the oven for 10 to 15 minutes, turning the skewers over after 5 minutes, until the peppers are soft and the chicken is cooked through. To make sure the chicken is properly cooked all the way through see what dad says on page 47.

# HEALTHY CRISPY ONION RINGS

I'm always trying to find healthy ways of making my favourite foods that aren't normally very healthy. These onion rings are dipped in really light Japanese breadcrumbs then baked in the oven rather than deep-fried – perfect for dipping and dunking.

**Serves 8**

4 onions

300ml buttermilk

300g Panko breadcrumbs

2 tbsp mixed dried herbs

1 tsp paprika

1 tsp pepper

Salt

1. Heat your oven to 200°C/180°C fan/gas mark 6. Line a couple of baking trays with foil.

2. While the oven is heating up, peel the onions and slice each one into 1cm wide slices then pop out the individual rings.

3. Pour the buttermilk into a mixing bowl and add the onion rings. Stir them gently to coat them all over. In a second mixing bowl, mix together the breadcrumbs, herbs, paprika and pepper.

4. Dip the onion rings in the breadcrumb mixture so they are well coated all over.

5. Put the coated onion rings on to the lined baking trays in single layers and cook in the oven for 20 to 30 minutes until golden and crisp.

6. Sprinkle with a little salt before serving.

### Dad says...

Panko are extra fine, dried breadcrumbs from Japan and chefs use them in the kitchen all the time to get a really crispy finish. It used to be difficult to get hold of them if you weren't working for a restaurant but these days you can buy them in all the major supermarkets.

# POPCORN CHICKEN AND PRAWNS

When you blitz popcorn it makes a great tasty, crunchy crumb for chicken and prawns. It's totally poptastic! These are also delicious with the kale and artichoke dip on page 81.

**Serves 4**

1 tbsp vegetable oil

100g popcorn kernels

100g dried breadcrumbs

Salt and pepper

2 eggs

350g diced chicken or 2 chicken breasts chopped up

250g peeled raw prawns

**For the Thousand Island dip**

3 small gherkins

2 spring onions

120g mayonnaise

4 tbsp tomato ketchup

1 tbsp Worcestershire sauce

1 lemon

2 tbsp flat-leaf parsley leaves

**Special kit list**

Food processor

1. Heat your oven to 200°C/180°C fan/gas mark 6. Line two baking trays with foil.

2. Put a large saucepan over a high heat and pour in the vegetable oil. When the oil is really hot (it will shimmer and start smoking; see my tip), add the popcorn kernels, give the pan a shake to coat them in the oil and put the lid on. After a little while the popcorn will start exploding in the pan! Wait until the pops slow down (about every 5 seconds) then take off the heat and leave to cool.

> **TILLY'S TIP:**
>
> A good way to know when the oil is ready for cooking the popcorn is to put 2 or 3 kernels into the pan. When they have all popped, the oil is at the right temperature.

> **Dad says...**
> Cooking popcorn is easy and fun, but, because it involves very high temperatures and flying pieces of hot corn, you need to be very careful – maybe get your mum or dad to help with that bit.

3. When the popcorn is cool, pour it into your food processor and blitz it to break it up roughly.

4. Put the blitzed popcorn into a bowl with the breadcrumbs and a sprinkle of salt and pepper and mix everything together.

5. Crack the eggs into a second small bowl and beat with a fork or whisk until it is well mixed.

6. Dip the chunks of chicken and the prawns into the egg one at a time then into the breadcrumb and popcorn mixture. Make sure they are coated all over. Keep one hand clean and dry to turn on the tap to wash your hands afterwards!

**7.** Put the coated chicken and prawns on two separate baking trays lined with foil and put them into the oven. Remove the prawns after 10 minutes and the chicken after 15 minutes.

**8.** While the chicken and prawns are cooking, chop the gherkins for the dip into small pieces with a large knife as you would cut nuts (see page 14). Slice the spring onions finely.

**9.** Put the mayonnaise, ketchup and Worcestershire into a mixing bowl and stir together. Add the chopped gherkins and spring onions to the bowl, squeeze in the lemon juice and stir again.

**10.** Chop the parsley leaves with a knife or in a mug with a pair of scissors (see page 14) and mix into the dip.

**11.** Put the dip into a bowl and serve with the crispy chicken and prawns.

## TILLY'S TIP:

These are great little tasty bites for a movie night! Why not serve them in popcorn bags for a real cinema experience?!

IT'S TOTALLY POPTASTIC!

BE PATIENT – THE LONGER YOU LEAVE THESE RIBS COOKING, THE STICKIER AND TASTIER THEY WILL BE

# CRAZY STICKY RIBS

Everyone loves these sticky ribs! They take a while to cook but the oven does all the hard work for you and the house will smell so amazing that your friends and family will start annoyingly hanging around the kitchen waiting for them to be ready.

**Serves 4**

1 onion

2 garlic cloves

2 tbsp olive oil

½ tsp chilli flakes (optional)

1 tsp fennel seeds

110g dark soft brown sugar

600g tomato ketchup

110ml dark soy sauce

1kg rack of pork spare ribs

Salt and pepper

1. Heat your oven to 150°C/130°C fan/gas mark 2.

2. While the oven is warming, peel and roughly chop the onion (see page 13). Then peel and crush the garlic in a garlic crusher.

3. Place a frying pan over a medium heat until it is hot, then add the olive oil, onion and garlic. Fry for 4 to 5 minutes or until the onion has softened.

4. Add the chilli (if using), fennel seeds and brown sugar and cook, stirring, for a further 1 to 2 minutes until the sugar has melted.

5. Add the tomato ketchup and soy sauce and stir everything together. Bring to the boil, then reduce the heat and simmer for 10 minutes, until the sauce thickens up.

6. Put the ribs into a deep-sided roasting tray and pour over the sauce.

7. Cover the tray with foil and put it into the oven for 2 hours, then increase the oven temperature to 180°C/160°C fan/gas mark 4, remove the foil and cook for 30 to 45 minutes more.

8. Once cooked, remove the tray from the oven and let the ribs cool down so they are not too hot to handle before serving.

9. Serve with lots of paper napkins because sticky fingers are guaranteed!

# BASKETBALL CALZONE PIZZAS

These look brilliant and taste good too. I made them for the basketball players when we hung out with them on the beach in L.A. and they couldn't get enough!

The dough needs to prove for an hour before you can use it.

### Serves 4

### For the pizza dough

280ml warm water (see what dad says, opposite)

1 x 7g sachet of dry yeast

480g plain flour

1 tsp salt

Olive oil, for greasing the bowl

### For the tomato sauce

1 onion

1 garlic clove

1 tbsp olive oil

$1/2$ tsp dried oregano

Salt and pepper

1 x 400g tin of chopped tomatoes

1 tbsp flat-leaf parsley leaves

1 tbsp basil leaves

### To assemble the basketball calzone

$1/2$ red pepper

$1/2$ green pepper

Flour, for dusting

120g grated mozzarella

8 slices of pepperoni

1 egg

### Special kit list

Stand mixer (not essential but will make things much easier!)

### To make the pizza dough

1. Pour the 280ml warm water into a mixing bowl then add the yeast. Stir gently to mix everything together. Put the bowl to one side for about 5 minutes to let the magic happen – the yeast should dissolve and start gently bubbling.

2. Put the flour and salt into the bowl of a stand mixer fitted with the hook attachment (or you can mix using your hands). Add the yeasty water and turn the mixer on. Mix until a smooth ball forms, which should take about 3 to 4 minutes.

3. Put the dough in a lightly greased large bowl then cover the bowl with cling film and leave the dough to prove in a warm place for about an hour or until the dough has doubled in size.

4. Knock back the dough (see my tip) and keep it covered while you get everything else ready.

## TILLY'S TIPS:

Knocking back the dough means to pummel it with your fists to get rid of any big air bubbles. It is an essential part of the process and will mean your bread or pizza dough has a more even texture. It's a great stress reliever too!

There will be leftover pizza dough when you cut out your bases and lids so use it to decorate the tops of the calzones. You can use pastry cutters or cut out your own flowers, stars, animals, faces, letters etc. I made them look like basket balls but use your imagination!

## To make the tomato sauce

1. Start by peeling and finely chopping the onion (see page 13) and peeling and crushing the garlic clove in a garlic crusher.

2. Heat the olive oil in a medium-sized saucepan over medium-low heat. When it's hot, add the chopped onion, garlic, oregano, salt, pepper and the chopped tomatoes. Put the lid on and leave to bubble for about 10 to 15 minutes, until it has thickened up a little.

3. While the sauce is cooking, chop the parsley and basil leaves with a large knife or in a mug with a pair of scissors (see page 14).

4. When the sauce has thickened, stir in the parsley and basil and take off the heat. Leave to cool.

### Dad says...

The warm water activates the yeast and gets it working but be careful not to use water that is too hot as it will kill off all the living organisms that make it work. If the water is too cold, those properties won't be activated. Officially, the ideal temperature is 38°C if you want to be precise!

## To assemble the calzone!

1. Heat your oven to 200°C/180°C fan/gas mark 6. Line a large baking tray with baking paper.

2. While the oven is heating up, pull out the seeds from the pepper and cut the flesh into thin slices for putting in your pizza.

3. Sprinkle your work surface with a little flour and roll or stretch out half the dough with your hands until it is about 0.5cm thick.

4. Use a 16cm round pastry cutter to cut out 4 circles (like basketballs!) and place them on the lined baking tray. (If you don't have a large cutter, carefully cut around a small plate.)

5. Top each dough circle with heaped tablespoons of tomato sauce. Spread the sauce out with the back of the spoon but leave a clear tomato-free ring around the edge.

6. Top with a few sliced peppers, the mozzarella cheese and a couple of pepperoni slices.

7. Roll out the rest of the dough in the same way and cut out 4 more circles. Put these 4 circles of dough on top of the covered bases and press the edges together with a fork so the filling is sealed inside.

8. Now to make them look like basketballs! Roll some of the leftover dough into little worms and use this to make decorations on top of the calzone, like the lines on a basketball.

9. Separate the egg, keeping the yolk in a small bowl or mug (see my tip on page 180), and whisk the yolk. Remember to wash your hands if you get any raw egg on your fingers. Brush the yolk on top of the calzones to help them get a golden crispy top as they cook.

10. Bake for 15 to 20 minutes until golden brown on top.

# CALIFORNIAN COOLER RASPBERRY LEMONADE

Fruity, fizzy and lemonady – this is just what you need after a hot day at the beach or sunbathing in the back garden. The combination of sharp lemons and sweet fruit is totally zingy and refreshing.

**Serves 8**

250g fresh raspberries, plus an extra handful for serving

250g caster sugar

8 lemons

1 apple

Ice cubes (optional)

1. Put the raspberries in a large saucepan with the sugar and 250ml water. Place the pan over a low heat and simmer until the sugar has dissolved. Remove the pan from the heat and allow the liquid to cool.

2. Cut the lemons in half and use a lemon squeezer to extract as much juice as you can.

3. Push the cooked raspberries through a fine sieve into a bowl so that you have a lovely smooth raspberry syrup without any seeds.

4. Pour the cooled syrup into a large jug and add the lemon juice. Stir them together then pour in a litre of water to dilute it.

5. Ta da! Home-made raspberry lemonade! Pour it into glasses with ice cubes, if using, and top with apple stars (see my tip) and fresh raspberries.

## TILLY'S TIP:

To make apples stars, slice an apple horizontally and take out any pips, then use a star pastry cutter (or any other shaped one) to press out a star. Super easy and so pretty!

**Dad says...**

Roll the lemons on the worktop with your palm, pressing down quite hard, before you cut and squeeze them – you will get more juice per lemon.

# HOW TO TAKE GREAT FOOD PICTURES FOR YOUR BLOG

Sharing pictures of what you cook online is almost as good as sharing it in real life!

**Natural light rocks.** All photographers are obsessed with natural light and it's no wonder – electric light and camera flashes can make colours look funny and your food won't look very appetising. So instead of turning the lights on, try to photograph your food by a window or even outside in the garden.

**Cook with colour.** I always like food to look bright and appealing with lots of different colours – it means it tastes really good but also that the pictures are great. If something is brown or beige, sprinkle herbs over the top or serve it with a colourful side dish or salad to make it look more interesting.

**Think about the background.** Food doesn't always have to be photographed on the kitchen table. Use fun backgrounds, painted floorboards, tablecloths, put plates on the grass, etc. Also, putting a well-placed knife and fork, napkin, glass or serving spoon in the picture can help give a shot atmosphere but . . .

Dad and I cook together in the kitchen a lot – he's always looking over my shoulder!

I LOVE TAKING PICTURES OF THE FOOD I COOK – LOOKING BACK AT THEM GIVES ME INSPIRATION FOR NEW RECIPES.

**. . . Keep it simple** – too much clutter and busy patterns can detract from the food which should always be the star. It's all about balance.

**Forget perfect.** Nobody will care if your cake is a bit wonky or your piping is scruffy as long as it looks really tasty.

**Think before you post.** Is your beans on toast for tea really interesting enough to take a picture of? If you want people to come back to your blog for more, only shoot the interesting things you cook and eat, not your breakfast cereal.

**Follow the professionals.** Look up the names of food photographers in cookbooks that you like, then follow them on Instagram. They are taking pictures of food all day every day and they know all the tricks.

The photographer who took the photos for this book has done such a fantastic job! Thanks, Jemma!

Me taking a selfie with my macarons!

# COOKING OUTSIDE

## barbecues, campfires and car engines?

This is from when I entered a barbecue competition at Long Beach in California and my family came to cheer me on! There were so many amazing people taking part, it was such an honour to be involved. And the whole place smelled like delicious smoky meat — YUM!

Dad's fancy plating at the beach barbecue!

Dad loves a barbecue and we've had some brilliant ones down on the beach in L.A. — although sometimes he doesn't let anyone else take over the grill!

Awesome burgers with surprise cheesy centres!

On the TV show, we cook outside all the time, mainly because we are often near the sea and it is so fun to have picnics and barbecues on the beach. It also helps that we spend lots of our summer holidays in L.A. where the weather is warm and sunny all the time. I love it in America but there is something really special about Cornwall, too. English beaches are amazing – the weather is obviously less predictable, but some of my favourite picnics have been wearing hoodies and raincoats as it drizzles on a soggy beach!

Dad absolutely loves barbecuing, so wherever we are, whatever the weather, if there's a chance to light up the grill, he does. He interferes with my cooking all the time but it's almost impossible to keep him away when I'm barbecuing. He can't help himself!

I've also cooked on an open fire and on camping stoves. One of the coolest things I did for the TV show was enter a big American barbecue competition in Long Beach, California. I went head to head with some really crazy characters who were really loud and whacky. I won sixth prize for my pulled pork sandwich and was given a set of golden tongs – dad was so jealous!

But this chapter isn't just about cooking on bonfires and barbecues, it's more about the type of food that you cook this way. It's the street food of America, like pulled pork rolls and burgers – really satisfying meaty food with big, smoky flavours. Of course, you don't have to cook on an open fire to follow these recipes – you can cook them all in your kitchen at home and they will taste *almost* as good. There's less risk of being rained off too. . .

My 'party in a pot' clam bake.

# HEAD TO PAGE 124 FOR SOME TIPS ON COOKING WITHOUT A KITCHEN

# BIG BOLD CHEESY BURGERS

The burgers need to sit in the fridge for at least an hour so they don't fall apart when you cook them.

I like recipes that have a twist so my burgers have a secret cheesy centre which no one knows about until they bite into them!

**Serves 4**

120g Cheddar cheese

600g beef mince

1/2 tbsp garlic powder (or you can use a crushed garlic clove instead)

Splash of Worcestershire sauce

Salt and pepper

2–3 tbsp vegetable oil

**To serve**

1 beef tomato

1/2 head of soft lettuce

Sliced gherkins

4 burger buns (seeded, plain or brioche rolls), sliced in half

Ketchup, mustard, mayonnaise or your favourite relishes

1. Cut the block of cheese into 4 chunks, each about 5cm long.

2. Put the mince, garlic powder and Worcestershire sauce into a large mixing bowl and season with salt and pepper. Mix it together with clean hands until the mince is soft and can easily be formed into shapes.

3. Divide the mince into 4 chunks and press a piece of cheese into the middle of each one. With wet hands, mould the mince into burger shapes, hiding the cheese inside, then put them on to a clean tray or plate. Always wash your hands when you've been handling raw meat.

4. Put the tray or plate into the fridge for at least an hour to rest (but no more than 24 hours) – this will help the burger to hold its shape when cooking.

5. Light your barbecue or heat your oven to 180°C/160°C fan/gas mark 4.

6. Brush the burgers with the oil (or rub the oil on lightly with your fingers).

7. If you are barbecuing the burgers, put them straight on to the grills when the flames have completely died away and the coals are at their hottest. Cook them for about 4 to 5 minutes on each side until brown and crispy. If you are cooking the burgers in the oven, put them on to a baking tray lined with baking paper and put the tray in the oven for 15 to 20 minutes until the meat is nice and brown. You can test if they are cooked by slicing into one – the juices should be clear. Just be careful not to cut into the middle or else the cheese will leak out!

8. While the burgers are cooking, slice the beef tomato. Pull the lettuce leaves apart, keeping them whole.

9. Serve the burgers in the buns with the lettuce leaves, tomato and gherkins and sauce them up with ketchup, mustard, mayonnaise or any other relishes you like. When everyone bites or cuts into the burger, the melted cheese will ooze out – burger heaven!

## TILLY'S TIP:

You could add diced onion, spices or fresh or dried herbs to the beef mince to make them extra tasty.

SURPRISE!

# PULLED PORK SANDWICHES

**MAKE AHEAD ALERT**

The pork takes 6 to 7 hours to cook so it's not one for straight after school when you're hungry!

I cooked this pulled pork at a BBQ competition in California – it has a prize-winning sauce with a super secret ingredient! The pork is cooked for a long, long time so you can literally pull it apart rather than cut it up with a knife. As most people won't have a big covered grill in their back garden, like the American pit masters(!), you can cook it in your oven and then finish it off on the barbecue for a smoky flavour, or just cook it in your home oven for a taste of the hot deep South when it's raining outside!

**Serves 6**

### For the pulled pork

1 tbsp salt

1 tbsp freshly ground pepper

3 tbsp light brown sugar

2 tbsp paprika

2 tbsp garlic powder

1.25kg boneless pork shoulder, cut in half across the middle (cutting the pork shoulder in half helps it cook more quickly)

### For the BBQ sauce

1 onion

3 garlic cloves

1 tbsp vegetable or sunflower oil

1 tbsp English mustard powder

150g light brown sugar

450g passata

1 tbsp molasses

2 tbsp yeast extract

120ml cider vinegar

1 tbsp Worcestershire sauce

2 tbsp brown sauce

1 Earl Grey tea bag brewed in 230ml of boiling water ← **SECRET INGREDIENT!**

### To serve

6 burger buns (seeded, plain or brioche rolls), sliced in half

Coleslaw

Sliced gherkins

BBQ Baked Beans (see opposite)

1. Start by preparing your pork. Mix together the salt, pepper, brown sugar, paprika and garlic powder and rub the mixture all over the pork pieces with clean hands. Leave the pork to sit for at least an hour but, for the very best results, overnight in the fridge. Always wash your hands after handling raw meat.

2. While the rub is working its magic, make the BBQ sauce: peel and chop the onion (see page 13) then peel the garlic and crush in a garlic crusher.

3. Put a large saucepan over a medium heat and add the oil. When it is hot, add the diced onion and crushed garlic and cook for about 5 minutes until soft and translucent, then add the mustard powder and stir together.

4. Weigh out and add the rest of the ingredients to the saucepan with the cup of tea. Bring up to the boil. As soon as the sauce is boiling, remove from the heat.

5. When you are ready to cook the pork, heat your oven to 150°C/130°C fan/gas mark 2.

6. While the oven is heating up, put the pork pieces into a large roasting tray and cover with **half** of the BBQ sauce (use the remaining sauce for the BBQ Baked Beans, opposite). The sauce will seem a bit runny but don't worry about that.

7. Cover the roasting tray with foil and put it into the oven for 6 to 7 hours until the pork is completely falling apart. Use a fork to test that the meat comes away from the bone easily. When the pork has half an hour left to cook, make a start on your BBQ Baked Beans.

8. Remove the pork from the tray and place on a large plate. Carefully, and making sure to use oven gloves to protect your hands from the hot dish, pour all the sauce into a saucepan and bring it to the boil. Allow it to bubble and simmer away for about 15 minutes, until it coats the back of the spoon – it should be a little bit thinner than ketchup.

9. While the sauce is thickening, begin pulling the pork apart using two forks – it should come apart very easily.

10. Mix the sauce with the shredded pork so that it is pretty saucy and wet.

11. Toast the buns and stuff each one with pulled pork, coleslaw and gherkins. Serve with the BBQ Baked Beans.

**TILLY'S TIP:**

The sauce makes enough for both the pork and the beans, but halve the ingredients for the sauce if you're only making the pork.

# BBQ BAKED BEANS

SUPER EASY PEASY

These are my smoky home-made baked beans which make a change from the regular kind once in a while. The sauce comes from cooking the pulled pork but you can also make it from scratch (see my tip). Make them ahead and reheat on the campfire!

**Serves 6–8**

4 rashers of streaky bacon

2 x 400g tins of pinto or haricot beans

The reserved half of the BBQ sauce from the Pulled Pork Sandwiches recipe, see opposite (approximately 450–500ml)

Salt and pepper

1. Start by chopping the bacon into small pieces. You can use a knife for this but scissors are even easier. Always wash your hands after handling raw meat. Drain and rinse the beans in a colander.

2. Put a large frying pan over a medium heat and add the bacon. Cook until the bacon is crispy, which takes about 5 minutes. (See what dad says on page 64 about why you don't need to add any oil.)

3. Add the beans and the reserved BBQ sauce from the pulled pork recipe to the pan and bring it up to a simmer so it is gently bubbling.

4. Cook at a low simmer for about 20 minutes, until sauce has thickened and is coating the beans nicely.

5. Season with salt and pepper before serving with the pulled pork sandwiches.

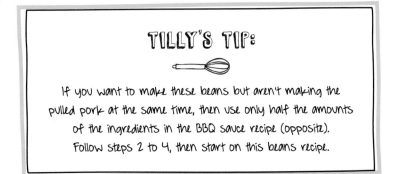

**TILLY'S TIP:**

If you want to make these beans but aren't making the pulled pork at the same time, then use only half the amounts of the ingredients in the BBQ sauce recipe (opposite). Follow steps 2 to 4, then start on this beans recipe.

# SAUSAGE WHEEL

When we were in L.A., I got the chance to make my own sausages! It's not something you'd do every day but it's so much fun and the results were totally delicious.

This was a real work out for my arms!

**Serves 6**

6 garlic cloves

½ bunch of sage

50g Parmesan cheese

1kg pork mince

100g rolled oats

Pinch of salt and pepper

1 tbsp paprika

1 tbsp vegetable or sunflower oil, for frying

Natural sausage casing – you can buy this online from specialist suppliers

**Special kit list**

Sausage maker (see my tip)

If barbecuing, 2 long skewers (if they are made of wood, soak them for at least 20 minutes in water)

## TILLY'S TIP:

If you don't have a sausage maker at home – it's not exactly essential kit! – fit your sausage casing on to stem of a funnel and spoon a little of the sausage meat into the funnel, pushing it down gently as you go with the handle of a wooden spoon. It will take longer but the sausages will still taste just as good.

1. Light your barbecue or heat your oven to 200°C/180°C fan/gas mark 6.

2. While the barbecue or oven is heating up, weigh out and prepare your ingredients: peel and crush the garlic cloves in a garlic crusher.

**3.** Pull the sage leaves off the stalks and chop them super fine with a large knife or in a mug with a pair of scissors (see page 14).

**4.** Grate the Parmesan cheese, using the fine side of the grater, and being careful not to grate your fingers!

**5.** Put the pork mince into a large mixing bowl (or in the bowl of a stand mixer with a paddle attachment). Add the rolled oats, grated Parmesan, crushed garlic, salt, pepper, paprika, chopped sage and 2 tablespoons of water.

**6.** With clean hands (or in your stand mixer), mix everything together thoroughly. Always wash your hands after handling raw meat.

**7.** Break off a small piece of the mixture and fry it in a small frying pan with a little oil. Taste it to check that the seasoning and flavours are as you like them. Add a little more salt, sage or paprika if you like.

### Dad says...

Sausages need some sort of filling like oats or breadcrumbs to keep them moist, otherwise all the juices run straight out when you're cooking them.

### TILLY'S TIP:

I think this is my favourite combination of flavourings for home-made sausages, but you could also experiment with using different herbs — like chopped flat-leaf parsley or chopped chives — and you could even add in some chilli flakes if you like things a bit hotter!

8. Following the instructions on the sausage maker, fit the casing onto the nozzle and fill the sausage casing with the pork mixture. If air bubbles or pockets form, use a skewer to punch a hole in the skin to let the air out.

Making sausages is DEFINITELY easier if you can get someone to help you!

9. Form one long sausage and coil it into a wheel on a baking tray lined with foil and greased with a little oil.

10. If you are barbecuing the sausage wheel, use 2 skewers to secure the wheel, so stick one all the way through then stick the other one through at right angles to make a cross. When the flames have completely died away and the charcoals are at their hottest, put the sausage wheel on to the barbecue and cook for 10 to 15 minutes on each side until golden brown all over.

11. If you are cooking the sausage wheel in the kitchen, put the baking tray into the oven for 25 to 30 minutes until cooked through.

TOTALLY DELICIOUS!

# BEACH CLAM BAKE

Clam bakes are really popular in America, especially if you live by the sea. I call it a 'party in a pot' because all the ingredients are cooked together in one big saucepan, which is perfect for when you are cooking on the beach. You can, of course, cook this on a regular stove but the view isn't quite as good . . .

## TILLY'S TIP:

Fresh, healthy clams should have closed shells before you cook them. If any of them are open, give them a little tap – if they close up, they are still alive and good for eating but if they don't close, throw them away. Then if any of the clam shells don't open during cooking, throw them away too.

**Serves 4–6**

400g chorizo sausage

2 celery sticks

2 onions

3 garlic cloves

1kg small new potatoes

4 corn on the cob or 8 half cobs

2 red peppers

2 tbsp tarragon leaves

Drizzle of vegetable or sunflower oil

3 tbsp white wine vinegar

1.5 litres vegetable stock

1 bay leaf

1.5kg clams in their shells, cleaned

600g raw prawns in their shells, heads removed (or you can use 500g peeled raw prawns)

Salt and pepper

1. Start by chopping the chorizo into chunks. Then slice the celery stalks on the diagonal into similar sized chunks. Peel the onions and cut them into quarters, then peel the garlic cloves and crush them in a garlic crusher.

2. Wash the new potatoes and chop them in half.

3. Peel the corn on the cob if they are still in their leaves. If you have whole cobs, cut them in half in the middle to make 8 half cobs.

4. Cut the peppers in half, remove the seeds and slice into thick strips.

5. Chop the tarragon leaves with a large knife or in a mug with a pair of scissors (see page 14).

6. When all your ingredients are prepared, put a large saucepan over a medium heat and add a little drizzle of vegetable oil. When it is hot, add the chorizo and cook for about 5 minutes, stirring it around from time to time.

7. When the chorizo has begun to release its oil, add the celery, onions, red pepper and garlic and cook for about 5 minutes.

8. When the celery and onions begin to soften, add the white wine vinegar and stir the vegetables with a wooden spatula to deglaze the pan, which is when you add a liquid to help scrape all the delicious crispy bits off the bottom of the pan. Then add the vegetable stock, the bay leaf and the halved potatoes. Cook for 10 minutes until the potatoes start to soften, then add the corn cobs for 5 minutes.

9. Finally add the clams and prawns and simmer for a further 5 minutes – you can tell when the clams and prawns are cooked because the clam shells open up and the prawns turn pink. Remove the pan from the heat, season with salt and pepper and stir in the chopped tarragon leaves.

10. Use a big ladle to serve the seafood, veggies and broth in large soup or pasta bowls. Serve with garlic bread (see page 156) for mopping up all the tasty juices.

# LEMON AND GARLIC FISH PARCELS

SUPER EASY PEASY

This way of cooking fish is so easy that we managed to do it on the engine of our car! It's just as scrummy cooked on the barbecue or even in the boring old oven . . .

**TILLY'S TIP:**

We cooked this in the bonnet of our car one day when we all forgot the coal for the barbecue! We all thought Dad was mad for suggesting it, but it worked out really well!

**Serves 4**

2 garlic cloves

2 lemons

25g dill

75g butter, at room temperature

Salt and pepper

4 x 150g white fish fillets with the skin on (cod, haddock, pollock, sea bass etc.)

**Special kit list**

4 pieces of foil (approximately 25cm square)

1. Light the barbecue or heat your oven to 200°C/180°C fan/ gas mark 6.

2. While the barbecue or oven is heating up, peel the garlic cloves and slice them as finely as you can.

3. Chop one lemon in half and squeeze out all of the juice. Cut the other lemon into thin slices.

4. Finely chop half of the dill with a large knife or in a mug with a pair of scissors (see page 14) and leave the rest as sprigs.

5. Lay a square piece of foil (about 25 x 25cm) on your work surface and spread it with some of the butter.

**6.** Scatter over a quarter of the garlic slices, some dill sprigs and season with salt and pepper. Lay a fish fillet on top, skin-side down.

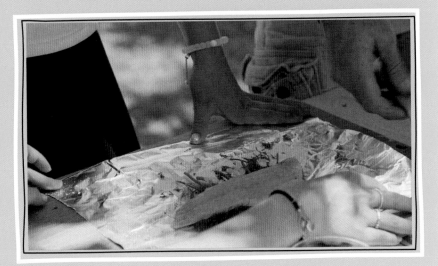

# IF YOU DON'T LIKE DILL, YOU CAN ADD CORIANDER, SPRIGS OF THYME OR PARSLEY, OR BASIL LEAVES

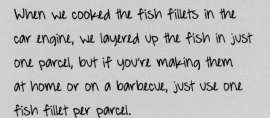

**7.** Pour a little of the lemon juice over the fish, sprinkle with some chopped dill, then lay lemon slices on top. Pour over a tablespoon of water and top with some more butter.

When we cooked the fish fillets in the car engine, we layered up the fish in just one parcel, but if you're making them at home or on a barbecue, just use one fish fillet per parcel.

### Dad says...
The thicker the fillet of fish the longer it will take to cook so if you have thin fillets such as sea bass or sole, cook them for 10 minutes and if they are thicker and meatier such as cod or haddock, leave them in the oven for 5 minutes more.

I've cooked outside in lots of places, but I think the car engine is definitely the weirdest!

8. Fold the foil over the fish to create a loose parcel and seal it round the edges so the juices don't leak out. Repeat this for each of the fillets.

9. If you are using a barbecue, wait until the flames have completely died away and the charcoal is at its hottest then put the parcels on to the grill for 10 to 15 minutes.

10. If you are in the kitchen, put the parcels on to a baking tray and put the tray into the oven to cook for 10 to 15 minutes. To check whether the fish is cooked, carefully open one of the parcels to see whether the fish is opaque and flakes easily when pressed gently with a fork. If this isn't the case, the fillets will need a bit more cooking.

11. When they are cooked, open the parcels and transfer to plates. The water and butter will have created a yummy sauce to spoon over the top. Sprinkle with any dill you have left over before serving.

WE ALL DOUBTED DAD AT FIRST BUT THE FISH PARCELS TASTED TOTALLY DELICIOUS! HIGH FIVE!

# CAMPFIRE RATATOUILLE

Once you've chopped all the veg for this ratatouille, all you have to do is mix them together with olive oil, herbs and garlic and let them cook in the fire – it's as simple as that. If you're stuck at home, you can also cook this in the oven with the added bonus that there is not much washing up. Magic.

## TILLY'S TIP:

I cooked this on our Wild West adventure in the edges of a bonfire. Use long tongs to put the parcels where it is hot but not flaming for 10 to 15 minutes - gently shake every so often. Once cooked, remove and leave them until they are cool enough to handle.

**Serves 4**

2 courgettes

1 medium aubergine

1 green pepper

1 red pepper

4 medium tomatoes

1 onion

1 garlic clove

2 tbsp flat-leaf parsley leaves

2 sprigs fresh thyme

4 large basil leaves

3 tbsp olive oil

Salt and pepper

1. If you're using your oven, heat it to 190°C/170°C fan/gas mark 5.

2. While the oven is heating up, get prepping those vegetables. Cut off and throw away the ends of the courgettes and aubergine then cut into 2–3cm cubes and put into a large mixing bowl.

3. Chop the peppers in half and pull out the seeds. Cut the flesh into cubes and add them to the courgettes and aubergine.

4. Roughly chop the tomatoes and put them into the bowl, seeds and juice as well.

5. Peel and chop the onion into small pieces (see page 13). Peel and chop or crush the garlic in a garlic crusher.

6. Chop the parsley leaves with a large knife or in a mug with a pair of scissors (see page 14). Pull the leaves off the thyme sprigs and roughly tear the basil leaves.

7. Add all the herbs to the bowl together with the olive oil and a little salt and pepper and stir everything together well.

8. Tear off 4 large pieces of foil and lay them out on your work top.

9. Divide the mixed vegetables between the foil pieces then wrap them up tightly, scrunching the foil edges together to make sure that everything is trapped inside.

10. Put the foil parcels on to a baking tray and put the tray into the oven to cook for 20 to 25 minutes or until the vegetables are all cooked.

11. Remove the tray from the oven and leave the parcels to cool until they are not too hot to handle. When cool, open up the foil, being careful to avoid the escaping steam, and serve with steaks, sausages or chicken or on their own, sprinkled with grated Cheddar cheese.

YUM!

# BANANAS IN PYJAMAS

I love bananas, especially when they are stuffed with peanut butter, chocolate chips and mini marshmallows and cooked so that everything melts together – beyond delicious.

**Serves 6**

6 bananas

6 tbsp crunchy peanut butter

175g chocolate chips

50g mini marshmallows

1. Heat your oven to 200°C/180°C fan/gas mark 6 or light the barbecue.

2. Using a small knife, cut out a strip of the banana peel all along the top of one side, so you have a window into each one, then cut a slit in the banana inside.

3. Spread a tablespoon of peanut butter inside each banana then cram as many chocolate chips and mini marshmallows on top of the peanut butter inside the banana as you can.

4. Wrap each whole banana tightly in foil individually and oven cook or barbecue for 10 minutes until the chocolate and marshmallows have melted and become gooey. Open one up and have a peek to make sure the banana is soft and the toppings are melted.

## TILLY'S TIP:

You can also put the foil-wrapped bananas into the hot coals of a fire and leave them until you are ready to eat them but make sure you use tongs with really long handles to put them in and take them out of the fire. Be careful!

They may look a bit mushy but they're absolutely delicious!

# COOKING WITHOUT A KITCHEN

We Ramsays love a barbecue! Any excuse and you'll find us barbecuing down at the beach or in the back garden, but compared to some of the crazy places we have cooked, a barbecue seems quite tame!

**Campfire cooking.** You can wrap things up in foil and cook them in the embers of the fire, or even in the warm ashes – but be very careful, as it will be extremely hot! And, of course, it's always fun to cook sausages or marshmallows on the ends of sticks!

**Things you can cook on an open fire:**
BBQ Baked Beans in a camping saucepan (see page 107), Lemon and Garlic Fish Parcels (see page 116), Campfire Ratatouille (see page 120), Bananas in Pyjamas (see page 123), jacket potatoes and corn on the cob wrapped in foil.

**Spade steaks!**

◉ If your spade has a wooden handle, soak it in water for half an hour before you put it in the fire so that it doesn't burn. Wash the metal end thoroughly at the same time.

Lean Machine Chicken Skewers (see page 53) are great for beach barbecues!

- Sterilise the spade by sticking it into the flames of the fire for at least 10 minutes – this will make it safe to cook on.

- Marinate your steaks for 30 minutes before you cook them (I used a mixture of Worcestershire sauce, soy sauce, mustard powder, lemon juice and salt and pepper) or else you can just rub them with a little oil and season with salt and pepper.

- You'll need a pair of long-armed tongs to put the steaks on to the spade when it is really hot. You'll hear it sizzle! Hold the spade just above the flames and, depending on how thick they are, cook your steaks for about 3 to 4 minutes before flipping over with the tongs then cook for 3 to 4 more minutes on the other side. If they're really thick, they may need a bit longer.

- Remove the steaks from the spade and leave to rest for at least 5 minutes before tucking in . . .

- Give your spade a really good wash down afterwards.

Tin foil parcels and campfire saucepans make cooking outside fun!

COOKING ON THE CAR ENGINE WORKED REALLY WELL WHEN WE WENT ON OUR FISHING TRIP AND FORGOT THE COAL FOR THE BARBECUE! WE CALLED IT A CARBECUE – GEDDIT?! DEFINITELY MAKE SURE YOU KNOW WHAT YOU'RE DOING BEFORE YOU ATTEMPT THIS ONE THOUGH!

# FEEDING THE FAMILY

crowd-pleasers for your own bunch

Mmm! Super cheesy enchiladas that I made for mum and dad's twentieth wedding anniversary.

Chilli is Jack's favourite meal.

We're a super competitive family but we always celebrate together — usually round a table of food!

# HEAD TO PAGE 158 FOR MY DOG BISCUIT RECIPE — PETS ARE FAMILY TOO!

In the summer we love to eat together in the garden.

When you're the youngest child in a noisy family of six, you really have to shout to get noticed. Instead of shouting, I started cooking . . . it is easier to get attention by producing a really tasty dinner for everyone than it is jumping up and down, making a lot of noise all the time! When yummy smells start to fill the house, everyone is suddenly interested in what I'm up to and they appear like magic to get a taste.

You might have noticed that Ramsay family life is always running at full speed. We're all really busy with school, sports, travelling, working and shooting the TV programme. It can be really crazy but we try to sit down for meals together whenever we can. It's the time when we can catch up and check in with each other and it's always really fun. The food is almost as important as the family time – there are always clean plates, even though no one stops talking for very long!

We mostly all like eating the same things at home. Holly is definitely the fussiest – she will only eat super healthy food – and Jack likes things much spicier than anyone else. Generally, though, we eat the same classic family dishes that everyone else does – lasagne, chilli con carne, fish pie etc. I have also included some of my favourite side dishes in this chapter like courgette fries, corn on the cob and garlic bread because they will turn your family meals into proper feasts. Just make sure that you get everyone to help with the washing up . . .
Yes, that includes you, Jack!

Cheesy, bacon corn on the cob.

Slam dunk delicious meatballs!

# MEATY LOADED LASAGNE

As well as the two different types of mince in the sauce, I also add grated carrots and courgettes to make it even more chunky and rich. Then there's my secret ingredient – maple syrup – which gives it an amazing smoky sweetness. It's a family favourite for a reason!

**Serves 8**

**For the meat sauce**

1 onion

3 garlic cloves

1 small courgette

1 small carrot

500g pork mince

500g beef mince

Salt and pepper

2 tsp fresh thyme leaves

2 x 400g tins of chopped tomatoes

2 tbsp maple syrup

**For the cheesy sauce**

200g strong Cheddar cheese

50g unsalted butter

150ml whole milk

150ml crème fraîche

**To put it all together**

150g Cheddar cheese

50g Parmesan cheese

250g fresh lasagne sheets

1 tbsp flat-leaf parsley leaves

**Special kit list**

An oven-proof dish (approximately 34 x 22cm)

1. First, make the meat sauce. Peel and roughly chop the onion (see page 13), then peel and crush the garlic cloves in a garlic crusher.

2. Top and tail the courgette then grate the flesh, being careful not to grate your fingers. Top and tail and peel the carrot and then grate that too.

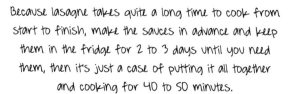

## TILLY'S TIP:

Because lasagne takes quite a long time to cook from start to finish, make the sauces in advance and keep them in the fridge for 2 to 3 days until you need them, then it's just a case of putting it all together and cooking for 40 to 50 minutes.

Dad's always trying to 'help' me in the kitchen! He's got great advice but we don't always agree on everything! ➤

**2.** Place a large heavy-bottomed frying pan over a medium-high heat. When it is hot, put the pork mince into the pan. Break the mince down with a wooden spatula or spoon as it cooks and keep stirring it until it is all well browned. Remove the pork mince from the pan and put it in a bowl (or a colander set over a bowl to drain off the juices). Cook the beef mince in the same way, then remove that from the pan as well, and add it to the cooked pork mince.

**4.** Add the chopped onion, crushed garlic and salt and pepper to the hot pan with the fresh thyme and grated veg. Give it a good stir and cook for a few minutes until the onions are soft.

**5.** Return the meats to the pan and stir again, then pour in the tinned tomatoes and maple syrup, stir and bring up to the boil. Turn the heat down to medium and leave to bubble away for about 30 to 40 minutes, until the liquid has reduced and it's a good thick consistency.

**6.** Heat your oven to 180°C/160°C fan/gas mark 4.

**7.** While the oven is warming up, grate the Cheddar cheese for the sauce, being careful not to grate your fingers. Grate the Cheddar and Parmesan cheeses for the topping, too, but keep them all in separate piles. Put the butter for the sauce into a small non-stick saucepan and place it over a medium-low heat. When the butter has melted, add the milk and cook for a couple of minutes. Then whisk in the crème fraîche and grated cheese. Cook gently until the cheese has just melted, then remove from the heat and leave to cool a little. It will thicken up as it cools – leave it to cool until it coats the back of a spoon.

8. Spread a large spoonful of the cheese sauce across the bottom of an oven-proof lasagne dish, about 34 x 22cm. Follow this with a layer of lasagne sheets, then 1/3 of the meat sauce. Cover this with a spoonful of white sauce and then more pasta sheets, tearing them to the right size if you need to. Repeat these layers – meat, white sauce, pasta – until the dish is full, making sure you end with a layer of pasta. Spread on the rest of the white sauce.

9. Top with the grated Cheddar and the grated Parmesan and put the dish into the oven for 40 to 50 minutes until the cheese has melted and everything is piping hot and bubbling.

10. Serve with parsley leaves sprinkled on top.

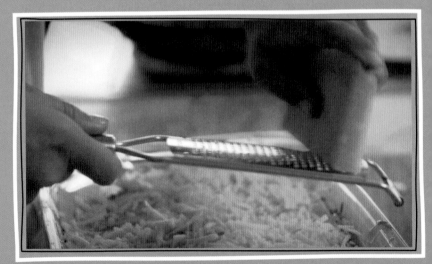

# ANY FISH PIE

This is called Any Fish Pie because, guess what, you can make it with any fish and it tastes equally good. In Cornwall, I made it with hake and lobster but you can use cod, haddock, salmon, pollock, etc.

**Serves 4–6**

**For the mashed potatoes**

1.5kg white potatoes

100g butter

200ml semi-skimmed milk

**For the pie filling**

4 spring onions

4 tbsp flat-leaf parsley leaves

150g Cheddar cheese

50g butter

175g frozen peas

1 tsp Dijon mustard

150ml semi-skimmed milk

150ml crème fraîche

450g selection of fish and seafood that has been skinned and chopped into large pieces, e.g. haddock, salmon and peeled prawns

Salt and pepper

**Special kit list**

Flame-proof casserole dish (approximately 25–30cm wide and 8–10cm deep)

1. Heat your oven to 200°C/180°C fan/gas mark 6.

2. Peel and cut the potatoes into quarters then put them into a large saucepan. Cover them with cold water and put the pan over a medium heat. When the water is boiling, turn down to a simmer and let the potatoes cook for 15 to 20 minutes until they are very soft.

3. Drain the potatoes in a colander, then put them back into the pan and mash them with a potato masher. Add the butter and milk to the pan and mash again until the potatoes are lovely and smooth.

4. While the potatoes are cooking, slice the spring onions into small rings. Then chop the parsley with a large knife or in a mug with a pair of scissors (see page 14).

5. Grate the Cheddar cheese, being careful not to grate your fingers!

6. Place the flame-proof casserole dish over a medium heat and add the butter for the filling. When it has melted, add the spring onions and fry for a minute or so.

7. Add the peas and the mustard and cook for another minute, stirring.

8. Add the milk and crème fraîche and gently simmer for 5 to 10 minutes until it thickens a little bit. Then add the cheese and give it a good stir.

9. When the cheese has melted, add the pieces of fish and cover them with the sauce. Stir in the chopped parsley and remove from the heat. Season with a little salt and pepper and stir again.

10. Spoon the mash on top of the fish mixture and spread it out to cover the whole top. Use a fork to make a wavy pattern on the top to look like the ocean but don't press too hard so you don't push through.

11. Put the dish into the oven for 20 to 25 minutes until bubbling around the edges and crispy on top.

12. Serve in bowls with extra veg on the side. How warming is that?

# CORNISH SEASIDE SAUSAGE SPAGHETTI

This is a classic Ramsay family dinner that we love eating on holiday in Cornwall. It is also really good for after school as it's quick to make and there are no fancy ingredients or skills involved.

**Serves 4**

1 small onion

2 garlic cloves

6 pork sausages

2 lemons

2 tbsp flat-leaf parsley leaves

400g dried spaghetti

Drizzle of vegetable or sunflower oil, for frying the pork

1/4 tsp chilli flakes (optional)

200ml chicken stock

100ml crème fraîche

Salt and pepper (optional)

## TILLY'S TIP:

Taste your sauce before adding extra salt – it might not need it because sausages are already quite salty.
I love chilli and add it to almost everything! But if your sausages are already spicy, you may not need the chilli flakes.

1. Start by peeling and finely chopping the onion with a sharp knife (see page 13) then peel and crush the garlic cloves in a garlic crusher.

2. With clean hands, remove the meat from the sausages by splitting the skin and turning them inside out. Always wash your hands when you have been touching raw meat.

3. Zest the two lemons with a fine grater – don't go too deep though as the pith under the skin is a bit bitter. Then, chop one of the lemons in half and extract the juice with a lemon squeezer. (The other zested lemon can be used for adding extra juice on the plate or for something else another day.)

4. Roughly chop the parsley with a large knife or in a mug with a pair of scissors (see page 14).

5. Put a large saucepan of salted water on to a high heat and bring it up to the boil. Once it is boiling, add the spaghetti, then reduce the heat so it is simmering and follow the packet instructions for the cooking time – normally around 11 minutes.

6. Put a large heavy-bottomed frying pan over a medium heat and add the oil. When it is hot, add the chopped onion, crushed garlic and chilli flakes if you are using them, and cook until the onions have softened.

7. Add the sausage meat to the pan and fry until golden brown. Like when you are cooking mince, you will have to break down the sausage meat with a spatula as it cooks.

8. Pour in the stock and allow it to bubble away until the amount of liquid has reduced by half – this will take about 6 to 8 minutes.

9. When the stock has reduced, stir in the crème fraîche, lemon zest and juice and season with salt and pepper (see my tip). Cook for 2 minutes more.

10. Once cooked, drain the pasta and add it to the sausage sauce in the frying pan with a spoon of the pasta cooking water (see opposite what dad says about why you should do this). Give it a good stir so the sauce covers the spaghetti then serve with the chopped parsley scattered on top.

**Dad says...**

Always keep back a little of the pasta cooking water (about a tablespoonful) to mix in with the pasta – it is the magic ingredient that helps the sauce bind to the spaghetti and makes the whole dish more silky and delicious.

# SLAM DUNK MEATBALL SUBS

They're crazy about meatball sandwiches in the States, or subs as they call them, but you don't have to serve these ones in a sandwich if you don't want to. They're brilliant with spaghetti too.

**Serves 6**

**For the meatballs**

1 small onion

2 garlic cloves

2 tbsp flat-leaf parsley leaves

2 slices of stale white bread

75ml milk

1 egg

700g beef mince

Worcestershire sauce

1 tsp dried oregano

Salt and pepper

A drizzle of vegetable oil, for frying

**For the tomato sauce**

1 small onion

1 garlic clove

1 tbsp olive oil

1/2 tsp dried oregano

Salt and pepper

1 x 400g tin of chopped tomatoes

1 tbsp flat-leaf parsley leaves

1 tbsp basil leaves

**To serve**

150g Cheddar cheese

6 sub rolls

1. Heat your oven to 200°C/180°C fan/gas mark 6. Line a baking tray with foil.

2. While the oven is heating up, start the meatballs. Peel and finely chop the onion (see page 13) then peel and crush the garlic in a garlic crusher.

3. Roughly chop the parsley with a large knife or in a mug with a pair of scissors (see page 14).

4. Chop the crusts off the bread then put it into a bowl and pour over the milk. Wait for a couple of minutes for the bread to soak up the milk.

DID YOU KNOW THAT THEY ARE CALLED SUB ROLLS BECAUSE THEY LOOK LIKE SUBMARINES?!

**5.** Crack the egg into a small bowl or mug and beat with a fork or whisk. Remember to wash your hands if you get any raw egg on your fingers.

**6.** Put the mince in a large bowl and add the crushed garlic, chopped onion, beaten egg, chopped parsley, a few dashes of Worcestershire sauce, the dried oregano, salt and pepper and the soaked bread.

**7.** With clean hands, mix all the ingredients together until well combined.

**8.** With wet hands, form the mixture into 18 golf ball-sized meatballs. Put them on your lined baking tray. Always wash your hands when you've been handling raw meat.

9. Put the tray into the oven for 20 to 25 minutes until cooked all the way through (cut one in half after 20 minutes and if there is any pink inside, return them to the oven for another 5 minutes).

10. While the meatballs are cooking, make the tomato sauce. Finely chop the onion (see page 13) and peel and crush the garlic clove in a garlic crusher.

11. Heat the olive oil in a medium-sized saucepan over a medium-low heat. Add the chopped onion, garlic, oregano, salt, pepper and the chopped tomatoes. Put the lid on and leave to bubble for about 10 to 15 minutes, until it has thickened up a little.

12. While the sauce is cooking, chop the parsley and basil leaves with a large knife or in a mug with a pair of scissors (see page 14).

13. When the sauce has thickened, stir in the parsley and basil and take off the heat.

14. Grate the Cheddar cheese, being careful not to grate your fingers!

15. When the meatballs come out of the oven, put them into the tomato sauce and carefully stir them until they are coated all over.

16. Preheat the grill to high.

17. Split the sub rolls down the middle, keeping them attached along one edge, and put 3 meatballs into each one. Spoon over some of the tomato sauce and sprinkle over the grated Cheddar.

18. Put the rolls on to a baking tray and put them under the hot grill for about 5 minutes until the cheese melts and starts to bubble.

DEELISH!

# TILLY'S ALL-AMERICAN CHILLI

This is Jack's desert island meal – he loves it so much that we have it all the time at home. We usually eat it with rice or jacket potatoes but in America they serve it with cornbread which I've now learnt to make (see opposite). It's really easy and delicious and goes brilliantly with the spicy, meaty chilli.

**TILLY'S TIP:**

Megan likes her chilli with sour cream, Holly likes it sprinkled with chopped spring onions, Jack covers his in cheese and I love it with all three on top of each other! To make sure everyone gets to eat it the way they like it, put bowls of different toppings and extra chilli sauce on the table so everyone can make their own dream chilli.

**Serves 4**

1 onion

4 garlic cloves

Drizzle of vegetable or sunflower oil, for frying

450g beef mince

225g tomato purée

1 x 400g tin of chopped tomatoes

250ml chicken, beef or vegetable stock

1 tbsp chilli powder

2 tsp ground cumin

Salt and pepper

1 x 400g tin of kidney beans (drained)

Sour cream, grated Cheddar cheese and sliced spring onions, to serve

1. Start by peeling and roughly chopping the onion (see page 13) then peel and crush the garlic cloves in a garlic crusher.

2. Drizzle the oil into a large saucepan and place over a medium-high heat. When it is hot, add the chopped onion and crushed garlic and cook until soft.

3. Add the mince to the pan and use a wooden spatula or spoon to break the mince into smaller bits and keep it moving around the pan until it is all browned.

4. Stir in the tomato purée and cook for about 5 minutes before pouring in the tinned tomatoes. Let it bubble together.

5. Pour in the stock and add the chilli powder and ground cumin then season with salt and pepper and give everything a really good stir. Bring up to the boil and then turn down the heat so that the chilli is gently simmering. Leave to simmer for 30 to 40 minutes, stirring from time to time to check that it isn't drying out (if it is, add a little more stock or water).

6. Stir in the kidney beans and cook for 10 minutes until warmed through.

7. Serve with the cornbread opposite and top with sour cream, cheese and spring onions etc. (see tip).

# WHY DO THEY CALL IT CHILLI WHEN IT TASTES SO HOT?

# CALIFORNIAN CORNBREAD

Instead of serving chilli with rice or baked potatoes like we do in the UK, the Americans make fresh cornbread to go with it. It's made from ground-up corn so is naturally sweet and has a really great texture – more like a cake than a bread really. It's easy to make and you can eat it on its own, with the chilli opposite or with hearty soups or stews.

## Serve 4–6

55g butter

140g plain flour

140g polenta (cornmeal)

2 tsp baking powder

2 tbsp sugar

Pinch of salt

2 eggs

284ml pot of buttermilk

100ml milk

## Special kit list

20 x 20cm baking tin (at least 5cm deep)

1. Heat your oven to 200°C/180°C fan/gas mark 6.
2. Put the butter into a small saucepan over a low heat to melt.
3. When it has melted, pour the butter into a mixing bowl with the flour, polenta, baking powder, sugar and a pinch of salt and stir everything together.
4. Crack the eggs into a separate bowl, then add the buttermilk and milk and whisk until well mixed. Remember to wash your hands if you get any raw egg on your fingers.
5. Pour the egg and milk mixture into the flour and polenta and mix everything together well.
6. Pour the cornbread mixture into a baking dish, about 20cm square and at least 5cm deep, and put it into the oven for 25 to 30 minutes until golden brown and cooked in the middle. Poke the centre with a skewer to check – if it comes out clean, the cornbread is cooked; if not, return to the oven for a few more minutes.
7. Cut the cornbread into squares and serve with the chilli opposite while it is still warm.

## TILLY'S TIP:

Cornbread is brilliant with chilli con carne but you can also serve it on its own or for breakfast spread with honey butter. Mix 100g of soft butter with a generous tablespoon of honey and slather it on the cornbread when it is fresh from the oven. It's a knockout combination.

CORNBREAD
+ CHILLI
= YUM!!

# BAKED GREEN FRIES

Everyone loves chips but we all know that they're not good for us so I've come up with chips you can eat without the guilt. The secret? Swap potatoes for courgettes, give them a nutty, crispy coating then bake don't fry them. Nailed it!

### TILLY'S TIP:

I sometimes sprinkle a pinch of paprika over the chips to give them a tasty smokiness.

**Serves 8**

8 medium courgettes

4 eggs

300g ground almonds

150g Parmesan cheese

Salt and pepper

Pinch of paprika (optional)

1. Heat your oven to 220°C/200°C fan/gas mark 7.
2. Top and tail the courgettes then slice each one into chip-sized batons.
3. Crack the eggs into a mixing bowl and beat them together with a fork or whisk until they are well mixed. Remember to wash your hands if you get any raw egg on your fingers.
4. Weigh out the ground almonds. Grate the Parmesan cheese, using the fine side of the grater, and being careful not to grate your fingers! Mix them together.
5. Line a baking tray with baking paper.
6. Dip the courgette chips in the egg, a handful at a time, and then in the almond mix, making sure they are well coated.
7. Put all the chips on to the lined baking tray in a single layer, then put the tray into the oven for 15 to 20 minutes, turning them over halfway through cooking, until the chips are golden brown and crisp.
8. Season with salt and pepper and paprika, if you are using it, before putting them on the table, but don't expect them to last long!

THESE ARE AMAZING DIPPED IN GARLIC MAYO OR KETCHUP

DIP-
TASTIC!

# CHEESY BEEF ENCHILADAS

This is a Ramsay family favourite because we all love Mexican food. Jack and Holly love it extra spicy but Meg and I like it less hot so we usually make it somewhere in the middle to please everyone.

## Dad says...

It is important that the frying pan is really hot when you are browning mince so that the meat gets a good colour. If the pan isn't hot enough, the mince will boil and turn an uninspiring grey. It won't taste as good either. A good way to tell whether the pan is hot enough is to toss in a tiny bit of mince and see whether it immediately sizzles. If it doesn't, wait a bit longer . . .

**Serves 6**

**For the sauce**

1 onion

1 tbsp vegetable or sunflower oil

1/2–1 tbsp chilli powder

1 tsp ground cumin

1 tsp dried oregano

2 x 400g tins of chopped tomatoes

**For the filling**

1 onion

1 garlic clove

1 fresh green chilli (optional)

1 tsp sunflower or vegetable oil

500g beef mince

Salt and pepper

**For the finished dish**

300g Cheddar cheese

6 soft corn or wheat tortillas

4 spring onions

60g pitted black olives

**To make the sauce**

1. Peel and roughly chop the onion (see page 13).

2. Place a large saucepan over a medium heat and add the oil. When it is hot, add the chopped onion and cook for about 5 minutes until soft and beginning to turn golden brown.

3. Add the chilli powder, cumin and oregano and stir over the heat for about 2 minutes or until everything begins to smell herby and spicy.

4. Stir in the tinned tomatoes and cook for 10 to 12 minutes until the sauce begins to thicken a bit.

**To make the filling**

1. Start by peeling and chopping the onion (see page 13) and peeling and crushing the garlic in a garlic crusher. Chop the chilli, if using (see page 13).

2. Put the oil into a large frying pan over a high heat and when it is hot, add the minced beef, chopped onions, crushed garlic and chilli, if using. Break the solid mince into small bits with a wooden spoon and cook for 5 to 10 minutes, stirring all the time, until the mince has all turned brown (see what dad says, above) and the onion has softened.

3. Season with salt and pepper and put to one side.

I made these enchiladas for the Mexican-themed party we threw for mum and dad's wedding anniversary. Cooking for my family is one of my favourite things to do!

## To assemble the finished dish

1. Heat your oven to 200°C/180°C fan/gas mark 6. Grate the Cheddar cheese, being careful not to grate your fingers!

2. Spread about 4 tablespoons of the tomato sauce on the bottom of a large oven-proof baking dish.

3. Lay out the tortillas and divide the mince between each one, piling it in a line in the middle, then roll the tortillas up so the filling is trapped inside.

4. Carefully put the tortilla rolls into the dish with the join underneath so they are snug and ready for cooking.

5. Pour the rest of the tomato sauce over the top then sprinkle with the Cheddar cheese.

6. Put into the hot oven for about 20 minutes until the cheese is all golden and bubbling and everything is really hot.

7. While the enchiladas are cooking, slice the spring onions and olives.

8. Remove the baking dish from the oven and scatter over the sliced spring onions and olives before serving.

A RAMSAY
FAMILY FAVOURITE

# CORN ON THE COB WITH CHEESE AND BACON

We ate corn on the cob with different toppings in the speed eating competition that was part of the Ramsay Games in L.A. and though there was a rumour that the girls' team were cheating (I'm not saying anything), I wolfed down every bit.

SUPER EASY PEASY

**Serves 4**

4 rashers of streaky bacon

4 corn on the cob

100g Cheddar cheese

60g butter

**Special kit list**

4 pairs of sweetcorn forks (see my tip)

1. Bring a large saucepan of water to the boil. While it is coming up to the boil, cut the bacon into small pieces with a sharp knife or pair of scissors. Remember to wash your hands after handling raw meat.

2. Put a frying pan over a medium-high heat and when it is hot, add the chopped-up bacon. Fry the bacon for about 4 minutes, stirring frequently until it is crisp all over. (See what dad says on page 64 about why you don't need to use any oil here.)

3. When the water is boiling, add the corn cobs and cook for 3 to 4 minutes.

4. Grate the Cheddar cheese, using the fine side of the grater, and being careful not to grate your fingers!

5. Put the cooked bacon bits on to a plate lined with a few sheets of kitchen paper to absorb the excess fat, and leave them to cool for a bit.

6. When the corn cobs are ready, take them out of the water and put them on a large serving plate. Put a knob of butter on each corn cob while they are still piping hot.

7. Sprinkle the corn cobs with the grated cheese and crispy bacon before serving with sweetcorn forks stuck in each end.

## TILLY'S TIP:

If you don't have those tiny little sweetcorn forks to put in each end of the corn, then use normal forks — they work just as well.

SWEETCORN ALSO GOES BRILLIANTLY WITH PESTO, CHILLI JAM OR JUST PLAIN WITH BUTTER

**Dad says...**

Don't be tempted to add salt to the cooking water for the corn – it will make it tough rather than juicy and sweet.

## Dad says...

As I am always telling Tilly, the better your ingredients are, the more delicious your cooking will be. This is especially true when it comes to tomatoes . . . no amount of marinating will make fluffy, tasteless tomatoes as good as sweet, ripe ones. Buy the nicest ones you can find.

# SUPER TOMATO MESS

This salad needs to marinate for 30 minutes before eating.

This is my take on the Italian bread and tomato salad panzanella. It is so super simple it doesn't even need any cooking, just a lot of squishing and squelching. Don't be afraid to get your hands messy . . .

**Serves 6–8**

1kg ripe vine tomatoes

1 cucumber

1 red onion

Handful of basil leaves

450g loaf of stale sourdough or other crusty bread

2 x 125g mozzarella cheese balls

3 garlic cloves

8 tbsp extra virgin olive oil

3 tbsp red wine vinegar

Salt and pepper

1. Roughly chop all the tomatoes and put them into a large bowl, making sure you catch all the seeds and juices, too.

2. Halve the cucumber lengthways then scrape out the seeds with a teaspoon. Slice the cucumber and add it to the tomatoes.

3. Peel, halve and finely slice the red onion then add it to the bowl.

4. Tear the basil leaves and put them into the bowl, too.

5. Tear the bread into bite-sized chunks with your hands then do the same with the mozzarella and add them to the bowl.

6. Peel the garlic cloves and crush them in a garlic crusher. Whisk together in a small bowl with the olive oil and red wine vinegar. Season with salt and pepper. Pour the dressing over the salad.

7. Now the fun bit: roll up your sleeves and mix everything together with clean hands, squishing and squelching until it is well mixed.

8. Cover the bowl with cling film and then leave the bowl on the work top so that everything marinates for at least 30 minutes before serving.

# I LOVE GETTING MESSY HANDS!

# HERBY GARLIC BREAD

This is one of my all-time favourite things . . . I could live off garlic bread, I love it so much. It is perfect for mopping up juices and sauces so goes really well with the clam bake on page 115, lasagne on page 130 or the sausage spaghetti on page 136.

### Dad says...

To make sure your garlic bread is crispy as well as soft and buttery, open the foil up after cooking and bake the bread for 5 minutes more to brown the top.

**Serves 8–10**

2 garlic cloves
Small bunch of flat-leaf parsley
230g soft butter
1 large bloomer loaf (about 400g)

1. Heat your oven to 200°C/180°C fan/gas mark 4.

2. While the oven is heating up, peel the garlic and crush it in a garlic crusher.

3. Pick the leaves off the parsley and finely chop them with a large knife or in a mug with a pair of scissors (see page 14).

4. Put the butter, crushed garlic and chopped parsley into a mixing bowl and mix everything together until your butter turns bright green.

5. Cut the loaf into slices with a bread knife but only cut three-quarters of the way through so the slices are all still attached to each other.

6. Lay a large piece of foil on your worktop and put the loaf on top. Use a spoon to fill the gaps between the slices with the garlic butter. Use it all up for really buttery bread – you can spread some on top too.

7. Tightly wrap the loaf in the foil and put on to a baking tray. Put the tray in the oven for about 15 minutes.

8. Remove the bread from the foil and serve.

### TILLY'S TIP:

If you like it super garlicky, add more cloves to the butter . . . guaranteed to keep vampires (and other people) well away!

A TILLY FAVOURITE!

# DOGTASTIC SNACKS FOR THE FAMILY PETS

We love animals in our family – we have two dogs, two cats, two fish and a tortoise, and they're all completely spoilt. I didn't want them to miss out on all the fun! I made these biscuits for Rumpole and Bruno and they loved them. I even managed to trick dad into putting one into his mouth! He spat it out even though they're totally edible, probably not that delicious for humans though . . .

Bruno and Rumpole

# HOME-MADE DOG BISCUITS

1 beef stock cube

350g wholemeal flour, plus extra for dusting the work top

1 egg

1. Heat your oven to 200°C/180°C fan/ gas mark 6. Line a baking tray with baking paper.
2. Put the stock cube into a measuring jug and add 125ml boiling water. Stir until the stock cube has completely dissolved.
3. Put the flour, egg and stock into a food processor and blend until it comes to a ball. You can also do this in a mixing bowl with a wooden spoon and a bit of elbow grease . . . Wash your hands if you get any raw egg on your fingers.
4. Dust your work top with flour then roll out the dough until it is 0.5cm thick.
5. Use doggy pastry cutters (such as bones and paw prints) to cut out the biscuits and put them on to your lined baking tray.
6. Cook in the oven for 30 minutes until golden brown.
7. Allow to cool completely before giving to your dogs . . .

## TILLY'S TIP:

Keep these dog biscuits in a tin or an airtight container for a week and treat your pooches with a special snack whenever they do something particularly cute!

WE TRICKED DAD INTO EATING A DOG BISCUIT!

# SNACKTASTIC TREATS

## awesome snacks for all the family

I love being active and don't like sitting still, but that means I often find myself needing a snack to give me an energy boost!

Sparkly popcorn cakes!

# GOLD MEDAL BISCUITS – TOTAL WINNER!

These Rescue Rings look like healthy doughnuts!

Mmm – these frozen yoghurt coolers are so refreshing on a hot day.

# MMMMM....

You can't be good all the time . . . there are moments – in between meals, after school, after practice – when only something sweet will do! This is where the recipes in this chapter come in . . . think biscuits, milkshakes and frozen yoghurt ice creams. Mmmmm . . . all delicious and not at all hard to make when you need a little boost.

Making your own snacks is really fun and a good way to get into cooking. Also, because you know exactly what goes into them, they are (a bit) better for you than shop-bought treats! If you're feeling a little nervous about cooking, start with something really easy like the Popcorn Cakes which are just like chocolate rice crispy cakes but made with popcorn – all you have to do is pop the corn and melt the chocolate. Making rocky road is also a piece of cake (geddit?!) because you don't have to bake it – you just leave it to set in the fridge. In fact, waiting for it to set hard enough to cut is the hardest bit about the whole recipe!

The most simple snacks are the ones that you don't actually have to cook at all, like the Rescue Rings on page 172. They are just apple slices slathered with chocolate spread or peanut butter and topped with nuts, raisins and freeze-dried fruits. Any combination goes! Putting different things together like this is my favourite thing about cooking and I'm always experimenting.  Just use your imagination with ingredients to find your own snack heaven – there are no rules!

Macarons . . . or macaroons?!

# HEAD TO PAGE 188 FOR TIPS ON ORGANISING THE PERFECT MOVIE NIGHT!

# GOLD MEDAL BISCUITS

How cool are these edible medals?! I made them for the first ever Ramsay Games. We're very competitive in our family so we don't need much of an excuse to set each other challenges but when it comes to baking, I'm clearly the winner!

MAKE AHEAD ALERT

The biscuit dough needs to rest for 1 hour before cooking and then the biscuits need to be completely cold before decorating.

**Makes 24**

225g soft butter

170g caster sugar

1 egg

350g plain flour, plus extra for dusting

100g icing sugar

1 vanilla pod, seeds scraped out (see dad's tip)

A little whole milk, if needed

**To decorate**

Edible gold food spray

White icing pens/tubes

Coloured ribbons

**Special kit list**

Stand mixer with the paddle attachment fitted (not essential but will make things much easier!)

Biscuit cutters – for medals use a 7–8cm ring

1. Put the soft butter into the stand mixer with the paddle attachment fitted then add the sugar. Mix the sugar and butter together until light coloured and creamy. You can do this in a mixing bowl with a wooden spoon but it is a lot more work!

2. Add the egg and flour and mix again thoroughly. Add the icing sugar and vanilla seeds and mix until it forms a ball. You might need to add a little bit of milk if it is a bit dry. Wash your hands if you get raw egg on your fingers.

3. Wrap the biscuit dough in cling film and chill in the fridge for 1 hour.

4. When ready to cook, heat your oven to 180°C/160°C fan/gas mark 4. Line a baking tray with a piece of baking paper.

5. While the oven is heating up, dust the clean work top with flour and roll out the dough with a rolling pin until it is 1cm thick. If you have time, chill again for 30 minutes.

6. Use a 7–8cm cutter to cut out circles and put them on to the lined baking tray at least 2cm apart.

7. If you are making medals, make a small hole in the top of the biscuits that is big enough to fit a ribbon through (I used a round piping nozzle).

8. Put the tray into the oven for 10 to 12 minutes until the biscuits are lightly golden all over.

9. Take the tray out of the oven and move the biscuits to a wire rack to cool before decorating.

**To decorate**

1. Spray the biscuits with edible gold food spray and allow them to dry on the wire rack.

2. Once the gold spray has dried, decorate with the white icing. Leave the icing to set for 5 minutes.

3. Just before serving, thread the ribbons through the holes that have been made and tie in a bow.

## TILLY'S TIP:

Try adding lemon, lime or orange zest or spices like ginger or cinnamon. Or replace 3 tbsp flour with 3 tbsp of cocoa powder.

## Dad says...

To get the tiny seeds out of a vanilla pod, all you have to do is split the pod with a sharp knife and open it out as much as you can. Then, use a knife or a spoon to scrape the inside from top to bottom. The black stuff you have gathered is hundreds of tiny seeds ready to make your biscuits taste amazing.

# POPCORN CAKES

The idea for these cakes came from a reader of my blog. I was having some friends over to celebrate the end of the summer just before going back to school and I was looking for ideas for pudding. Scarlett suggested popcorn cakes and this is the recipe I came up with. Everyone loved them on the day, so big thanks, Scarlett!

These cakes might not need any baking but they do take an hour to set in the fridge.

**Serves 8–12**

100g buttter

6 tbsp golden syrup

300g milk chocolate or white chocolate

80g plain popped popcorn (see my tip)

30g sprinkles

**Special kit list**

A heatproof bowl that fits over a saucepan

1. Put the saucepan on to the hob and add some water so that it comes about 5cm up the side of the pan. Bring the water up to the boil then turn the heat right down so it is simmering gently.

2. While the water is coming to the boil, line a baking tray with baking paper.

3. Chop the butter into small cubes and put it into the heatproof bowl. Add the syrup and break the chocolate into the bowl, then place the bowl on top of the saucepan. This will melt the butter and chocolate so stir them together as they melt. Make sure the bottom of the bowl isn't actually touching the hot water though, as this could cause the chocolate to overheat.

4. When the chocolate and butter have completely melted, remove the bowl from the heat and stir everything together. Add the popcorn to the bowl and stir again.

5. Spoon dollops of the mixture on to the lined baking tray or use your hands to make small cake shapes. Scatter with the sprinkles and put them into the fridge to set for at least an hour.

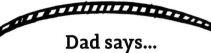

### Dad says...

Putting a glass bowl over simmering water to heat it gently is called a *bain marie*. The chocolate is melted by the steam heating the bowl rather than by heating the chocolate directly which may burn it. Do not let a single drop of water get into the chocolate or it may seize up. You can also melt chocolate in a microwave – see Tilly's instructions on page 176.

## TILLY'S TIP:

To make 80g popcorn, you will need 90g unpopped popcorn kernels. See page 86 for instructions for cooking popcorn.

# ROCKY ROAD TYRES

SUPER EASY PEASY

MAKE AHEAD ALERT

This takes 2 hours to set in the fridge.

This is my version of chocolate biscuit cake with lots of nuts and ginger biscuits instead of digestive biscuits. Apart from melting the chocolate, there is no real cooking as the 'cake' just sets in the fridge once you've mixed everything together.

**Makes 12-14 slices**

50g walnuts

10 ginger biscuits (about 100–120g)

340g dark chocolate

150g butter, at room temperature

55g toasted flaked almonds

40g raisins

25g mini marshmallows

25g shelled pistachios

1 tsp vanilla extract

**Special kit list**

A heatproof bowl that fits over a saucepan

1. Roughly chop the walnuts (see page 14) and crumble the biscuits into largeish pieces.

2. Put a saucepan on to the hob and add some water so that it comes about 5cm up the side of the pan. Bring the water up to the boil then turn the heat right down so it is simmering gently.

3. Break the chocolate into small pieces and put it into the heatproof bowl with the butter. Place the bowl on top of the saucepan until the chocolate and butter have completedly melted, stirring from time to time. Make sure the bottom of the bowl isn't actually touching the hot water though, as this could cause the chocolate to overheat. (See dad's advice on page 167.)

## TILLY'S TIP:

Of course you can use other biscuits and nuts — just make sure you use about the same weights as in this recipe otherwise the chocolate won't hold it all together.

THESE ARE CALLED 'TYRES' BECAUSE WE ATE THEM AT THE GO-KART TRACK!

4. Remove the bowl from the heat and stir in the ginger biscuit pieces, flaked almonds, raisins, marshmallows, walnuts, pistachios and vanilla extract until everything is coated in buttery chocolate. Allow to cool in the bowl for 20 minutes in the fridge – don't leave it for longer as it will set too hard!

**5.** Lay out a long piece of cling film on your work top and tip the chocolate mixture in a thick line down the middle to form a log. Roll up the log in the cling film and twist the ends tightly.

**6.** Put the log into the fridge and leave to set for at least 2 hours.

**7.** When it has set hard, remove the cling film and use a serrated knife to cut the log into rounds.

# THEY'RE WHEELIE NICE!

# RESCUE RINGS

I came up with these 'healthy doughnuts' when we were trying to think of ways to make money to protect sea lions in L.A. They're really easy to make – you don't need to do any cooking at all – and they sold like hotcakes because they look so tempting.

**Serves 6–8**

2 green apples

2 red apples

2 tbsp unsalted pistachios

100g chocolate spread

100g smooth peanut butter

2 tbsp freeze-dried strawberries

2 tbsp dried blueberries

2 tbsp flaked almonds

2 tbsp yoghurt-covered raisins

**Special kit list**

Apple corer (but see what dad says)

1. Carefully remove the core of the apples with a corer or small knife (see what dad says about how to do this).

2. Slice the apples in half across the middle and then each half in half again across the middle – so each apple ends up becoming four rings with holes in the middle.

3. Chop the pistachios with a large knife (see page 14) and put the pieces into a bowl.

4. Spread one side of the apple circles with either chocolate spread or peanut butter and lay them out on a plate.

5. To finish, sprinkle the apples with different combinations of the freeze-dried fruits, nuts and raisins.

## TILLY'S TIP:

Some of my favourite combinations are chocolate spread with pistachios and almonds, and peanut butter with yoghurt-coated raisins and freeze-dried strawberries, but get experimenting — you're in charge here!

### Dad says...

To core an apple with a small knife, put it on a chopping board with the stem at the top. Insert the knife about 2cm away from the stalk and cut straight down until the knife hits the board underneath. Pull the knife out and turn the apple a little bit then stick the knife in again. Repeat this, turning the apple as you go, until you have cut all around the core then push it out from the top.
Result: a core-free apple ready to go!

# MAGIC CHOCOLATE WANDS

The dough needs to prove for 30 to 45 minutes and the cooked wands need to cool.

These are made with a super simple bread dough that has only four basic ingredients – yeast, water, sugar and flour (the orange zest isn't essential but is really nice with the chocolate). So easy it's magic!

## Makes 8

1 x 7g sachet of dried yeast

2 tbsp caster sugar

110ml warm water (see page 93 for what dad says about how warm this water should be and why)

1 large orange

250g plain flour, plus extra for dusting

Vegetable or sunflower oil, for greasing the bowl

2 tbsp milk

1 tsp sea salt flakes (optional)

### For the chocolate coating

200g milk chocolate

70g white chocolate

Selection of sprinkles in different colours and shapes, to serve

### Special kit list

Stand mixer with a dough hook fitted (not totally essential but will make things much easier!)

A heatproof bowl that fits over a saucepan

1. Start by activating the yeast. Put the contents of the sachet into the bowl of your stand mixer and add the sugar and 110ml warm water. Mix them together a bit with a spoon then leave it alone for about 5 minutes, until the yeast begins to bubble. This is how you know that it is beginning to work.

2. While the yeast is doing its thing, take the zest off the orange with a fine grater, being careful not to go too deep – it's the zingy orange bits you are after rather than the bitter pith.

3. Next, add the flour and orange zest to the bowl and put it into the mixer fitted with the dough hook.

4. Turn it on and mix until it comes together in a dough – about 5 minutes. If the dough looks and feels a bit dry, sprinkle in a little more water until a ball forms and continue to knead for 5 minutes. If you don't have a stand mixer, you can do this by hand – it's a good work out!

5. Grease a medium-sized mixing bowl with a little oil and put the ball of dough into it then cover it tightly with cling film and leave it to prove in a draught-free area of the kitchen. The dough needs to prove for 30 to 45 minutes until it has doubled in size.

6. Heat your oven to 200°C/180°C fan/gas mark 6. Line a baking tray with a piece of baking paper.

7. Dust the work top with flour (mums and dads really love it when you start sprinkling flour around but hey, it has to be done if you don't want your dough to stick). Knock back the dough (see my tip on page 92) and turn it out on to the floury surface then knead it by hand for a few minutes.

8. Divide the dough into 8 pieces and shape each one into a 20cm long wand. Put the wands side by side on the lined baking tray, spaced apart.

IT'S GREAT FUN MAKING BREAD – KNEADING IT AND KNOCKING IT BACK. AND THIS IS A GOOD WAY TO GET STARTED. BEFORE YOU KNOW IT, YOU'LL BE MAKING YOUR OWN BAGUETTES, BUNS AND BRIOCHE!

IT'S MAGIC!

**9.** Brush the wands with the milk (or veg oil if you want to go dairy-free) and sprinkle with sea salt flakes if you want.

**10.** Put the tray into the oven to cook for 15 to 20 minutes until golden brown on top and hollow-sounding if you tap them on the underside.

**11.** Allow them to cool completely (on a rack with some baking paper underneath or directly on a sheet of baking paper) before decorating them, or the chocolate won't set.

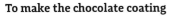

## To make the chocolate coating

**1.** Put a saucepan on to the hob and add some water so that it comes about 5cm up the side of the pan. Bring the water up to the boil then turn the heat right down so it is simmering gently.

**2.** Break the milk chocolate into small pieces and put it into the heatproof bowl then place the bowl on top of the saucepan until the chocolate has completely melted, stirring from time to time. Make sure the bottom of the bowl isn't actually touching the hot water though, as this could cause the chocolate to overheat. (See dad's advice on page 167.) You can also melt the chocolate in a microwave – see my tip for how to do this.

**3.** Pour the melted milk chocolate into a shallow tray (a baking tray works well) and dip the wands into the chocolate to coat them all over, leaving enough uncovered at one end so you can hold them. Put them on a lined baking tray. Sprinkle the wands with coloured sprinkles then leave them to set at room temperature.

**4.** While they are cooling, melt the white chocolate as above. Drizzle the wands with the white chocolate in a zig zag pattern.

**5.** Leave them to set for a few more minutes before serving.

# ICED YOGHURT SUPER COOLERS

These need to be frozen for 4 hours before eating.

These are sort of like mini upside down cheesecakes with the biscuit base on top. They're so good and so easy to make – such a refreshing snack for a sunny day. I made them for the basketball players we hung out with at the beach and they were perfect for cooling everyone down.

SUPER COOLER ANYONE?

Half time on the basketball court and everyone takes a break before my team romps to victory.

**Makes 9**

100g digestive biscuits

65g butter

150g fresh mixed summer berries,
e.g. strawberries, raspberries,
blackberries and blueberries

150ml milk

150g natural yoghurt

1 tbsp honey

**Special kit list**

Tray of 9 ice lolly moulds
(mine were 60ml each)

Blender or smoothie maker

1. Put the biscuits into a freezer bag and seal it. Wrap the bag
in a tea towel (to muffle some of the noise!) then smash the biscuits with
the rolling pin.

2. When the biscuits are all crushed up, pour them into a mixing bowl.

3. Next put the butter into a small saucepan and melt it over a low heat.

4. When it has melted, pour the melted butter into the bowl with the biscuit
crumbs and mix together with a wooden spoon.

5. Put about a tablespoon of the mix into the bottom of each ice lolly mould
and push down so it's firm and flat.

6. Put the berries into your blender with the milk, yoghurt and honey and,
with the lid safely on, blitz until smooth.

7. Pour the berry yoghurt on top of the biscuit base in the ice lolly moulds
and push a stick gently into each one. Put the moulds in the freezer for at
least 4 hours until it's frozen.

8. When you are ready to eat them, take the frozen iced yoghurt lollies out
of the freezer and leave them to melt a little bit before turning them out of
their moulds and eating.

# SUPER LIGHT MACARONS

Is it macaroons or macarons? Megan and I had a huge argument about this when I made them for the show. Mum had to get in between us! But who cares what they're really called – they taste amazing.

**Dad says...**

The cream of tartar is added to the meringues to help to stabilise them so they keep their volume when mixed with the ground almonds and icing sugar.

## TILLY'S TIP:

To separate egg whites from egg yolks, crack the egg on the side of a bowl or jug but don't pour everything into the bowl or jug. Instead, use the shell to keep the yolk back and let the white flood out into the bowl or jug. Each time you do this, pour the white into a second bowl before cracking your next egg; that way, if you do make a mess of it you have only wasted one egg rather than all of them. Use the egg yolks to make custard, mayonnaise or the lemon curd on page 198. Remember to wash your hands if you get raw egg on your fingers.

## Makes 12

120g ground almonds

250g icing sugar

4 egg whites (see my tip, opposite)

Pinch of cream of tartar

55g caster sugar

Raspberry jam for the filling

## Special kit list

Stand mixer with a whisk attachment fitted (not essential but will make things much easier!)

Piping bag and 1cm round nozzle

1. Using a sieve, sift the ground almonds and icing sugar into a mixing bowl to make them extra light and airy.

2. Put the egg whites into the mixing bowl of a stand mixer with a pinch of cream of tartar and whisk until soft peaks form. This is when the mixture is getting thick enough that when you pull out the whisk, the whites will form a little mountain but the very tip of it will flop over to one side.

3. When the whites are whipped to soft peaks, pour in the caster sugar while continuing to whisk until stiff peaks form. This is when that little mountain has a very sharp point with no flopping over.

# OR IF YOU'RE FEELING REALLY BRAVE...

4. Turn off the whisk and remove the bowl then carefully fold in the sifted almonds and icing sugar mixture with a spatula. The idea is to mix everything together but without knocking any of the air out of the egg whites. Be gentle and don't over mix it but make sure there aren't any streaks in the mixture.

5. Transfer the mixture to a piping bag fitted with a 1cm round nozzle.

6. Line a baking tray with baking paper or a silicone liner and pipe small round circles (about 4cm wide) in neat lines (about 2cm apart).

7. Leave the tray to sit out for at least 10 minutes to dry out. Heat your oven to 160°C/140°C fan/gas mark 3.

8. Put the tray of macarons into the oven and bake for 10 to 12 minutes, until they are just begining to turn light golden at the edges.

9. Remove the tray from the oven and leave the macarons on the tray to cool.

10. Once cool, carefully peel the macarons off the paper and spread half of them with raspberry jam and stick the other half on top to make a tiny jam sandwich.

# JUST LIKE OUT OF A BAKERY IN PARIS!

# CHOCOLATE AND PEANUT BUTTER MILKSHARE

I call this my milkshare because it's a giant milkshake that everyone can *share* – geddit? Pour it into a big jug and give everyone a straw so they can all drink the shake at the same time, unless you have a greedy brother like Jack in which case individual glasses are safer . . .

**Serves 6–8**

200g smooth peanut butter

3 scoops of vanilla ice cream

200ml chocolate milk

200ml milk

50g salted peanuts

**Special kit list**

Blender

1. Put the peanut butter, ice cream, chocolate milk and normal milk into a blender and blitz until smooth – make sure the lid is on really tightly!

2. Chop the peanuts with a large knife (see page 14). Make sure they are in small enough pieces that they will fit up your straws!

3. Pour the milkshake into a large glass bowl and sprinkle with chopped peanuts. Stick a straw in for each of the people sharing the drink. Alternatively, pour the shake into individual tall glasses.

PUT IT IN THE MIDDLE OF THE TABLE AND MAKE SURE EVERYONE HAS A STRAW!

# ICE CREAM SANDWICHES

These are no ordinary sandwiches . . .
Instead of using bread, I use croissants
dipped in a mixture of egg, sugar, vanilla
and cinnamon before frying them in butter –
so they are a bit like eggy bread which
I really love. But don't take them to a game
of kayak water polo like I did – the ice cream
melted and leaked everywhere!

**TILLY'S TIP:**

You could also do this
with slices of brioche or
doughnuts or even just plain
old bread. It's amazing
whatever you use.

**Serves 4**

4 croissants

4 eggs

75ml milk

1/2 tsp ground cinnamon

1/2 tsp vanilla extract

2 tbsp caster sugar

50g butter

4 scoops of vanilla ice cream

2–3 tbsp honey or maple syrup
(optional)

**For the cinnamon sugar**

75g caster sugar

1 tsp ground cinnamon

1. Start by slicing the croissants in half horizontally through the middle.

2. Crack the eggs into a mixing bowl and beat them with a fork or whisk
until well mixed. Remember to wash your hands if you get raw egg on
your fingers.

3. Add the milk, cinnamon, vanilla extract and sugar to the bowl and whisk
together until well mixed.

4. Put the croissant halves into the eggy mixture, allowing them to soak
in the liquid for 10 seconds.

5. Put the butter into a large frying pan over a medium heat and when it
starts to foam, cook the croissant halves for 1 to 2 minutes, then turn them
over and cook for 1 to 2 minutes more. You will probably need to do this in
a couple of batches.

6. While they are cooking, make the cinnamon sugar by putting the sugar
and cinnamon into a bowl and mixing it up. Simple as.

7. Spread the cinnamon sugar over a plate and when you take the croissant
halves out of the frying pan, put them onto the plate and then flip them over
so they are coated all over in the sugar.

8. Put the croissant bottoms on to plates and put a scoop of ice cream on
top, then drizzle with honey or maple syrup, if using, and put the croissant
tops on top to make a sandwich.

# HOW TO PULL OFF AN AWESOME MOVIE NIGHT

**Pick the right film.** Think about who is going to be watching the film with you – is it just your family or a group of friends? It's difficult to please everyone but you can try.

**Choose the film in advance.** Get everyone to vote on what they want to watch before they arrive so that you don't waste half the evening fighting over it. It will save so much time and you can get started quicker – which parents will like because it won't be too late when it finishes.

**Get comfortable.** Make sure there are enough chairs for everyone – six friends on one sofa just doesn't make for a relaxed, comfy evening! Get out the beanbags, mattresses and cushions to cover the floor, and rugs, too, if it's cold.

**Make your own drive-in.** In L.A., we built a screen in the garden with a sheet hanging off a wooden frame then projected a movie on to it. It was so much fun. Mum and dad drove up in a golf buggy!

**Be prepared.** It's no good having to pause the film to get food out of the oven or fridge or to make drinks for everyone. Do all the cooking in advance and put drinks in the middle of the coffee table so everyone can help themselves.

MOVIE NIGHT AND SNACKS – SOUNDS LIKE A PERFECT EVENING TO ME!

We made some poptastic music videos when we were in L.A. — they were so funny to watch! Move over Beyoncé, Til-yoncé is in the house!

**What's on the menu?** Keep the food simple and not sloppy, especially if it's dark as it can make a real mess. Tortilla Cups are perfect (see page 76) as are crisps, Healthy Crispy Onion Rings (see page 85), L.A. Nachos (see page 74), Slam Dunk Meatball Subs (see page 138), Rocky Road Tyres (see page 168), Rescue Rings (see page 172) and my cake pops (see page 206). Veggie Dogs (see page 48) are a nice twist on cinema hotdogs and a milkshare (see page 184) is always fun.

**Get popping.** There has to be popcorn. Even if you're full. Check out page 86 for how to make it, then make lots. Or if you can't decide between popcorn and chocolate, make Popcorn Cakes (see page 167) to please everyone. Or you could even try my Popcorn Chicken and Prawns on page 86 for an alternative move night popcorn experience!

# SWEET STUFF

puddings and cakes to die for

Watermelon was the perfect base for my sweet pizza — it looks just like tomato sauce! I topped it with chopped grapes for the olives and a pile of shredded coconut for the cheese!

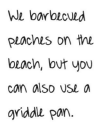

We barbecued peaches on the beach, but you can also use a griddle pan.

I love the POP in my Pop Power Chocolate Brownies!

Meringues are SO easy but they look really impressive.

I made a rainbow cake as a surprise for mum and dad's twentieth wedding anniversary — it has TWENTY layers inside!

I love baking because it's a bit like magic – if you mix the right combination of ingredients together and put them in the oven for the right amount of time at the right temperature, then wonderful things happen. It's also really fun, especially given all the opportunities to lick the spoon! I think that's a legitimate chef's perk, no?

You don't have to be a junior master chef to tackle the recipes in this chapter – they're mostly straightforward and easy. Some of them, like the Watermelon Pizza and the Grilled Summer Peaches, are really, really simple but others do take a bit more work – mainly the Roll Over Rover Cake on page 210 and the 20-layer Surprise Rainbow Cake on page 212, which will take quite a long time but is well worth the effort. Imagine everyone's faces when they cut in to it and see the rainbow layers . . .

My favourite pudding is definitely meringues. I love making them as much as I love eating them. They're so easy to cook – you just leave them in the oven for hours until they are really crisp on the outside and slightly chewy in the middle. They are particularly yummy with lemon curd and raspberries like on page 198 or crushed up in an Eton mess.

We always make birthday and anniversary cakes at home – it's the best way to celebrate and nothing says you care like a pile of home-made cupcakes or a brilliant cake. Getting good at baking also has the added advantage of making you really popular at home and at school. A good slice of cake is the way to almost anyone's heart!

**HEAD TO PAGE 216 FOR MY TIPS ON ICING AND DECORATING CAKES**

Don't forget the flake in your '99!

# WATERMELON PIZZA

This sounds a bit crazy but, trust me, it's totally awesome and, as puddings go, pretty good for you too. The watermelon slice serves as the base and the kiwis, apples and grapes (or whatever you like) are the toppings.

**Serves 8**

3 limes

120g caster sugar

1 apple

50g coconut flakes

1 kiwi

75g black or red grapes

75g green grapes

1 thick slice from the middle of a large watermelon or 2 thick slices from a smaller watermelon (use the rest to make watermelon juice by blitzing the flesh in a blender or smoothie maker and stirring in a handful of chopped up mint leaves)

**Special kit list**

Apple corer (not essential but will make things much easier – see what dad says on page 172 on using a knife instead)

1. Start by making a lime syrup to pour over the watermelon pizza when you serve it. Use a fine grater to zest one of the limes (being careful not to grate too deep – it's just the green bit you want, not the bitter white pith underneath). Cut all 3 limes in half and squeeze all their juice out.

2. Pour the lime juice into a small saucepan and add the zest, caster sugar and 120ml water. Stir everything together and put the pan over a low heat for about 4 minutes, carrying on stirring, until the sugar has totally dissolved.

3. Remove the pan from the heat and allow to cool.

4. While the syrup is cooling, carefully take the core out of the apple with a corer if you have one or a small knife if you don't (see page 172). Slice the apple into thin wedges. Roughly chop the coconut flakes.

5. Peel the kiwi fruit (see my tip), cut it in half lengthways and slice it into semi-circles. Cut all the grapes in half.

6. Put the thick slice or slices of watermelon on to a large plate or board then top with the apple and kiwi slices and scatter the grapes all over as if you were decorating a pizza. Top with the mozzarella – I mean coconut flakes!

7. Just before serving, pour the lime syrup over the watermelon and then cut it into wedges.

## TILLY'S TIP:

Peeling a kiwi with a spoon makes it really easy – just chop the top and bottom off the fruit and then, with the kiwi standing on one flat end, push the tip of the spoon in between the flesh and the skin, with the back of the spoon against the skin. Keep pushing until you reach the bottom then careful rotate the kiwi, gently prising the flesh away from the skin until you get back to where you started. Result: a naked kiwi fruit with zero wastage.

THE RED WATERMELON LOOKS LIKE TOMATO SAUCE!

# MAGIC '99 ICE CREAMS

This isn't really ice cream but it's still amazing and so clever, if I say so myself. You don't need an ice cream maker, just a good blender, and some waffle cones and chocolate flakes to serve. Dad thought it was so good that he gave it my first ever ten out of ten!

The bananas need to be in the freezer for at least 2 hours.

**Serves 4–6**

4 bananas

2 tbsp smooth peanut butter

150g frozen blackberries

4–6 ice cream cones

25g sprinkles

4–6 chocolate flakes

**Special kit list**

Blender or food processor

1. Peel and slice or break the bananas into thick pieces then put them into a freezer bag. Seal the bag and freeze for at least 2 hours until the banana is rock hard.

2. Put the frozen banana into a blender or food processor with the peanut butter and the blackberries and blitz until smooth – it should have the consistency of ice cream! Stop blending every so often and use a scraper to scrape down the insides.

3. Scoop some magic ice cream into the ice cream cones.

4. Dip the ice creams into the sprinkles so they are covered then stick in a flake. Hey presto – super quick cheat's ice cream!

## TILLY'S TIP:

You can use other frozen berries or cherries too or leave out the peanut butter and use chocolate spread instead. Experiment with different combinations but don't add any liquid otherwise it will be too runny to stay in the cones.

# LEMON MERINGUE SANDWICHES

Meringues take a really long time to make . . . they need to dry out for over 3½ hours.

I love meringues and they are one of my favourite things to bake. Once you have put the egg whites into the mixer, there's not much for you to do; just sit back and relax while the machine does all the hard work. Same goes for the cooking – once they're in the oven, you can get on with other things while they slowly dry out.

**Serves 4**

**For the meringues**

2 egg whites (use the yolks to make the curd below) (See page 180 for how to separate egg whites from egg yolks)

100g caster sugar

**For the lemon curd**

(or you can use shop-bought curd)

2 whole eggs

2 egg yolks (left over from the meringue)

1 large lemon

100g caster sugar

100g soft unsalted butter

2 tsp cornflour

About 20 raspberries, to serve

**Special kit list**

Stand mixer with the whisk attachment fitted (not essential but will make things much easier!)

**To make the meringues**

1. Heat your oven to 150°C/130°C fan/gas mark 2. Line a large baking tray with baking paper.

2. Put the egg whites into the bowl of the stand mixer and whisk until they are thick and foamy. You can do this with an electric hand whisk or by hand too. Remember to wash your hands if you get raw egg on your fingers.

3. Next, start adding the sugar a tablespoon at a time, whisking well between additions. Beat until all the sugar has been used up and the egg whites are super glossy and thick enough that when you pull out the whisk, the whites form a little mountain that has a very sharp point with no flopping over. This is called stiff peaks.

4. Use 2 tablespoons to spoon 8 mounds of meringue on to the lined baking tray. Use the back of a clean spoon or a palette knife to slightly flatten out the shapes, giving them a little twirl on top. They should be about 3cm high.

5. Put the tray into the middle of the oven and reduce the heat immediately to 140°C/120°C fan/gas mark 1.

6. After 30 minutes, turn the oven off and leave the meringues to dry out in the oven for 3½ to 4 hours.

## To make the lemon curd

1. While the meringues are in the oven, make the curd. Crack the whole eggs into a medium saucepan and add the 2 egg yolks left over from the meringues. Beat them together with a balloon whisk so they are well mixed. Remember to wash your hands if you get any raw egg on your fingers.

2. Use a fine grater to zest the lemon, being careful not to grate too deeply – it's only the yellow bit you want, not the bitter pith underneath. Then squeeze out the juice using a lemon squeezer.

3. Put the saucepan on to a medium heat then add the lemon zest and juice, sugar, butter and cornflour. Use a balloon whisk to mix everything together and keep whisking over the heat for about 7 to 8 minutes, until the mixture begins to bubble.

4. Once the mixture has become nice and thick, remove the pan from the heat, still stirring.

5. Put a sieve over a clean mixing bowl and strain the mixture through it to get a really glossy, smooth curd. Then leave it to cool and put it into the fridge until you are ready to use it.

A stand mixer is SO useful when making meringues as it means you don't have to do all that whisking by hand. You definitely don't need one though – you can always just build up those arm muscles!

## To assemble the meringue sandwiches

Peel the meringues off the baking paper and turn them upside down. Spoon lemon curd (you will have some lemon curd left over, which is delicious on toast!) on to four of them then put a ring of raspberries around the edges. Put the other four meringues on top and sandwich them together – you can use a splodge of lemon curd to help the lids stick if needed. Decorate with a single raspberry stuck on to the meringue with a dot of lemon curd.

THE WAY TO TELL WHETHER
THE EGG WHITES HAVE BEEN
WHIPPED ENOUGH IS TO TURN
THE BOWL UPSIDE DOWN OVER
YOUR HEAD — IF THEY FALL
OUT, YOU SHOULD HAVE
WHISKED THEM SOME MORE!!

# GRILLED SUMMER PEACHES

This is one of my favourite puddings ever. It's an easy one too, so much so that Megan and Holly made it on the beach when they gave me a day off from cooking. If they can cook it, anyone can!

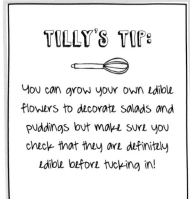

**TILLY'S TIP:**

You can grow your own edible flowers to decorate salads and puddings but make sure you check that they are definitely edible before tucking in!

**Serves 4**

4 ripe but firm peaches

1 tbsp olive oil

Salt and pepper

Handful of almonds

100g soft and creamy goat's cheese

2 tbsp honey

Fresh edible flowers like marigolds, Nasturtiums or pansies

1. Slice each peach in half, twist them apart and remove the stones.

2. Put the peach halves into a bowl then drizzle them with the olive oil and sprinkle with salt and pepper. Gently move the peaches around with clean hands so they are all coated.

3. Put a griddle pan or frying pan over a medium-high heat.

4. When the pan is hot, cook the peaches for 3 to 4 minutes on each side until a few grill lines appear and the fruits are beginning to soften.

5. While the peaches are cooking, chop the almonds into pieces with a large knife (see page 14).

6. Arrange the cooked peaches on a big serving plate. Leave them to cool for a little while before crumbling the goat's cheese on top.

7. Drizzle the peaches with honey, sprinkle with the chopped almonds and decorate with the edible flowers.

DRIZZLE WITH HONEY... TILL-ICIOUS!

# POP POWER CHOCOLATE BROWNIES

The brilliant thing about brownies is that you can make them your own by putting whatever you like inside. I've added sour cherries for an extra kick and sprinkled them with popping candy to make them super poptastic.

**Makes 8–12 brownies, depending on how big you cut them!**

115g butter, plus a little extra for greasing

300g caster sugar

225g dark chocolate

75g plain flour

Pinch of salt

1 tsp vanilla extract

75g cocoa powder

5 eggs

250g dried sour cherries

2 tbsp milk, if needed

100g popping candy

Edible glitter or sprinkles, to decorate

**Special kit list**

25 x 30cm brownie tin

A heatproof bowl that fits over a saucepan

1. Heat your oven to 180°C/160°C fan/gas mark 4. Grease and line a 25 x 30cm brownie tin with baking paper.
2. Put the butter and sugar into a mixing bowl and beat together using an electric hand whisk or by hand, until light and fluffy.
3. Next, melt the chocolate. Put a saucepan on to the hob and add some water so that it comes about 5cm up the side of the pan. Bring the water up to the boil then turn the heat right down so it is simmering gently.
4. Break the chocolate into small pieces and put it into a heatproof bowl. Place the bowl on top of the saucepan until the chocolate has completely melted, stirring from time to time. Make sure the bottom of the bowl isn't touching the hot water though, as this could cause the chocolate to overheat (see dad's advice on page 167). You can also melt the chocolate in a microwave (see my tip on page 176).
5. Pour the melted chocolate into the butter and sugar mixture and whisk to combine.
6. Add the flour, salt, vanilla extract and the cocoa powder and mix together.
7. Crack the eggs into a separate bowl and beat them with a fork or whisk until well mixed. Remember to wash your hands if you get any raw egg on your fingers. Stir the eggs into the chocolate mixture until mixed together.
8. Finally, gently stir through the sour cherries. If the mixture feels too stiff, loosen it with a couple of tablespoons of milk.
9. Pour the mixture into the lined tin, then put it into the oven to bake for 40 to 45 minutes until the brownies are coming away from the side.
10. Take the brownies out of the oven and leave to cool in the tin.
11. When cool, cut into big or small squares depending on how many people you are serving or how greedy you are feeling.
12. Sprinkle with the popping candy and edible glitter or sprinkles.

# SWEET POTATO CAKE POPS

The sweet potatoes need to be cooked and cooled before you can make the cakes. This will take about 1½ hours. The cake pops also need to firm up in the fridge for an hour.

I love putting unexpected ingredients into things so these cake pops are made with sweet potatoes. You can't really taste them but they add natural sweetness which when mixed with the dates means you don't have to add any extra sugar. There are other good things in these too like nuts, oats and coconut so they're virtually health food!

**Makes 24**

2 sweet potatoes (approximately 500g in total)

75g walnuts

75g soft dates without stones

125g rolled oats

125g ground almonds

¼ tsp ground cinnamon

Pinch of flax seeds

Pinch of sesame seeds

75g desiccated coconut

½ tsp vanilla extract

Icing sugar, if needed

400g milk chocolate or dark chocolate

**Special kit list**

8 cake pop sticks, skewers or lolly pop sticks

A heatproof bowl that fits over a saucepan

1. Heat your oven to 200°C/180°C fan/gas mark 6.

2. Put the sweet potatoes on to a baking tray and when the oven is hot, put them into the oven and cook for 45 minutes until soft. To test whether they are soft, carefully squeeze them gently through a tea towel – but be very careful of the hot oven!

3. When the potatoes are soft, take them out of the oven and leave them to cool completely.

4. While the potatoes are cooling down, chop your walnuts (see page 14) and dates up into small pieces and measure out the rest of the ingredients.

5. When the sweet potatoes are cool, slice them open and use a spoon to scoop the soft flesh out of the skins and into a large mixing bowl.

6. Add the oats, ground almonds, cinnamon, flax seeds, sesame seeds, coconut, chopped walnuts and dates and the vanilla extract and mix everything together until it forms a solid dough. If it is too wet, add a little icing sugar.

7. With your hands, break off chunks of the dough and roll them between your palms to make 24 balls. They should be about the size of ping pong balls.

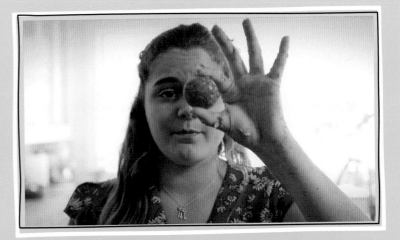

# I KNOW IT'S UNUSUAL TO USE SWEET POTATOES, BUT THEY REALLY DO TASTE DELICIOUS!

8. Put the balls on to a clean plate or tray then stick a cake pop stick, skewer or lolly stick into each one. Put the tray into the fridge for about an hour to firm up.

**9.** While the cake pops are chilling, melt the chocolate. Put a saucepan on to the hob and add some water so that it comes about 5cm up the side of the pan. Bring the water up to the boil then turn the heat right down so it is simmering gently.

**10.** Break the chocolate into small pieces and put it into a heatproof bowl then place the bowl on top of the saucepan until the chocolate has completely melted, stirring from time to time. Make sure the bottom of the bowl isn't touching the hot water though, as this could cause the chocolate to overheat (see dad's advice on page 167). Turn off the heat but leave the bowl over the pan. (You can also melt the chocolate in a microwave, see page 176.)

**11.** When the cake pops have firmed up, dip them in the melted chocolate to coat all over and allow them to set on a sheet of baking paper before scoffing!

(see dad's advice on page 167)

(You can also melt the chocolate in a microwave, see page 176.)

### TILLY'S TIP:

The lolly sticks are quite long so you might need to clear some space in your fridge so they can stand up without hitting the shelf above them.

I MADE THESE ➡ FOR OUR POPTASTIC DAY WHEN WE MADE OUR OWN MUSIC VIDEOS – THEY LOOK JUST LIKE XYLOPHONE STICKS OR MICROPHONES!

THEY'RE VIRTUALLY HEALTH FOOD!

# ROLL OVER ROVER CAKE

We Ramsays love our dogs almost as much as the crazy dog-owners in L.A. I made this chocolate roly poly to celebrate pets everywhere! See my tip for how to make the doggy decorations.

**TILLY'S TIP:**

If you want to add a dog's face and legs to the roly poly like I did, you will need to bake an extra sponge at the same time and cut out the shapes when it has cooled. Pipe on melted chocolate.

## Serves 8–10

4 eggs

110g caster sugar, plus extra for dusting

Seeds from 1 vanilla pod (see what dad says about getting the seeds out of a vanilla pod on page 165)

75g self-raising flour

### To decorate

200g milk chocolate

400g raspberry jam

### Special kit list

Swiss roll tin or baking tin with shallow sides (23 x 33cm)

A heatproof bowl that fits over a saucepan

Electric hand whisk (not essential but will make things much easier!)

1. Heat your oven to 190°C/170°C fan/gas mark 5. Line a 23 x 33cm Swiss roll tin with baking paper.

2. Put the eggs, sugar and vanilla seeds into a bowl and whisk until very light, fluffy and thickened – you can use an electric hand whisk or do it by hand. Remember to wash your hands if you get any raw egg on your fingers.

3. Using a fine-mesh sieve, sift the flour over the mixture and fold it in gently so you don't knock all the air out of it.

4. Pour the mixture into the lined tin and smooth it out with a spatula until evenly spread out.

5. Put the tin in the oven and bake the sponge for 10 to 12 minutes until just firm to the touch.

6. While your sponge cake is cooking, place a sheet of baking paper slightly bigger than the tin on to the work surface and dust with some caster sugar.

7. Flip the tin over so the sponge is on the baking paper, then peel the paper off the bottom of the sponge. Set aside to cool slightly – for about 5 minutes.

8. While the sponge is cooling down, melt the chocolate. Put a saucepan on to the hob and add some water so that it comes about 5cm up the side of the pan. Bring the water up to the boil then turn the heat right down so it is simmering gently.

9. Break the chocolate into small pieces and put it into a heatproof bowl then place the bowl on top of the saucepan until the chocolate has completely melted, stirring from time to time. Make sure the bottom of the bowl isn't actually touching the hot water though, as this could cause the chocolate to overheat (see dad's advice on page 167). Remove from the heat. You can also melt the chocolate in a microwave (see my tip on page 176).

10. When the sponge has cooled down a bit, spread it with the raspberry jam and roll the sponge tightly until you have a long log shape.

11. When it has completely cooled, cover the roly poly with melted chocolate using a palette knife or spatula and leave it to set at room temperature before serving with ice cream.

WOOF! WOOF!

# 20-LAYER SURPRISE RAINBOW CAKE

**MAKE AHEAD ALERT**

The cakes take an hour to cook and then have to be chilled completely before you can assemble and decorate the final cake. It also needs to be chilled for 2 hours before you put the final icing on later. It's an epic undertaking!

This cake takes a LOT of effort but looks so brilliant when you cut into it that it's totally worth it. People will have no idea that there is a rainbow inside! I made it for mum and dad's twentieth wedding anniversary – the cake and buttercream make up twenty layers for twenty years!

**You need to make 2 batches of the following so make sure to buy double the ingredients!**

350g soft butter, plus extra for greasing the tins

600g caster sugar

6 eggs

1½ teaspoons vanilla extract

450g plain flour

½ tsp salt

1 tbsp baking powder

360ml whole milk

5 different food colourings – red, yellow, green, blue and purple

Edible silver spray, to decorate

**Special kit list**

You will need 6 bowls for this cake! One very large one for the mix and 5 medium ones – one for each colour.

5 x 20cm cake tins – no more than 5cm high or they won't all fit in the oven at the same time

Stand mixer with a whisk attachment fitted

1. Heat your oven to 180°C/160°C fan/gas mark 4.

2. Put the butter and sugar into the bowl of a stand mixer fitted with the whisk attachment and beat for about 5 minutes until it's light and fluffy.

3. Add the eggs, 2 at a time, waiting until each set of eggs is fully mixed in before adding the next 2. Remember to wash your hands if you get raw egg on your fingers.

4. Next add the vanilla extract.

5. Sift the flour, salt and baking powder into the sugar and butter mixture, a bit at a time, and whisk until it is incorporated – when you have added a third of the flour, add half of the milk, then repeat until all the ingredients are in the mixing bowl.

6. Use a rubber spatula to scrape the sides of the bowl and mix one last time to ensure all the ingredients are fully mixed in. Scrape this into a very large mixing bowl.

7. Repeat with second batch in the stand mixer.

We threw mum and dad a surprise Mexican-themed party for their twentieth wedding anniversary. As well as this amazing cake, I also made the enchiladas on page 148.

8. Combine the two batches of cake batter in the very large bowl so that all the cake mix is together, then divide the mixture equally between 5 medium bowls – use scales for this if you want to be exact.

9. Add the different food colourings to the bowls a few drops at a time and mix them in so there are no streaks. Add more if you want more intense colours.

10. Grease the bottom and sides of the 5 cake tins with butter and put a circle of baking paper on the bottom of each one.

11. Pour a different-coloured cake mix into each cake tin.

12. Put the cake tins into the oven for 40 to 50 minutes. After 40 minutes, poke a skewer or toothpick into the centre of the cakes – if it comes out clean, the cakes are cooked but if not, return them to the oven for a little longer and check again in 5 minutes' time.

13. Remove the cakes from the oven and let them cool before carefully removing them from the tins. Wrap them in cling film and put them into the fridge or freezer to make sure they are completely cold before you trim and slice them.

14. While the cakes are in the freezer, make the buttercream icing using the method opposite. Cover the bowl with cling film until you need it.

15. When the cakes are completely cold, use a serrated knife to carefully trim away the edges, top and bottom, taking off small amounts at a time to remove the brown edges and reveal the colourful inside of the sponge cake.

16. Cut the cakes in half horizontally to give you two cake sponges of each colour.

17. Put a third of the butter icing into a separate bowl and re-cover the rest with cling film.

18. Put a small dollop of icing on to a cake stand to stick the first layer of sponge to the bottom.

19. Put one of the purple sponges on to the cake stand then start spreading icing on to the sponge, very thinly at first to press crumbs in place – this layer of icing is called the crumb coat. Then add a bit more icing to create a buttercream layer between the sponges.

20. Top this with one of the blue sponges and repeat with the crumb coat and icing layer.

21. Top this with one of the green sponges and repeat with the crumb coat and icing layer.

22. Top this with one of the yellow sponges and repeat with the crumb coat and icing layer.

23. Top this with one of the red sponges and repeat with the crumb coat and icing layer.

**TEN LAYERS OF CAKE PLUS TEN LAYERS OF ICING EQUALS TWENTY LAYERS! ONE FOR EACH OF THE YEARS MUM AND DAD HAVE BEEN MARRIED**

**24.** Then repeat all the layers again until the top final red layer. Cover the top with the crumb coat then cover the sides of the whole cake with crumb coat too.

**25.** Put the cake into the fridge to set and chill for about 2 hours.

**26.** Remove the cake from the fridge and use the remaining icing to cover the entire cake, top and sides. Use a palette knife to make it as smooth as possible.

**27.** Spray the whole cake with edible silver spray and serve to the delight and awe of everyone you know!

### For the buttercream icing

800g soft butter

1 tsp salt

2 tsp vanilla extract

1.75kg icing sugar

2 tbsp milk, if needed

### Special kit list

Stand mixer with a whisk attachment fitted

**1.** Put the butter and salt into your stand mixer fitted with the whisk attachment and beat until it is light and fluffy.

**2.** Add the vanilla extract.

**3.** With the mixer on low, sift in the icing sugar, a little at a time, until it is all mixed in – if it is a bit thick, add a little milk.

# MY CAKE AND BiSCUiT DECORATiNG TiPS

**The first question is: which icing?** Different icing works for different bakes. The main three are buttercream, fondant and royal icing.

**Buttercream** (mostly butter and icing sugar – see page 215) is perfect for covering and filling cakes and decorating cupcakes.

**Fondant icing** (usually bought ready made) is used for covering large celebration cakes and you can also roll it out and cut shapes out of it.

**Royal icing** (mostly egg whites and icing sugar) is good for pouring over cakes and for piping patterns, pictures and words on to biscuits and cupcakes, such as my Gold Medal Biscuits (see page 164).

**Make it smooth.** Use a palette knife to spread icing on top of a cake to make it nice and flat. If you don't have a palette knife, use a clean ruler – it works just as well!

**Twist the cake, not yourself.** When you are icing the sides of a cake, put it on to a cake stand or plate first and turn the stand or plate as you go, rather than trying to stretch over it to reach the back. It's so much easier and the finished cake will look more even too.

Icing biscuits is all about steady hands and plenty of practice!

This is the twenty-layer cake I made for mum and dad's anniversary – see page 212 for the recipe!

**Practise your piping.** Practise your stars, rosettes and flowers on a plate rather than on the finished cupcakes or cake. That way you can just scrape the icing up when you make a mistake and mix it back in with the rest of the icing when you're ready to start for real. The more you practise, the steadier your hand will be.

**Say it with sweets.** If your piping skills aren't quite good enough to write on the cake, you can still make it personal by spelling out the name, initials or age in smarties or jelly beans. I put a big T for Tana and a heart on mum's birthday cake and she loved it.

**Make a piñata cake.** Cut out the centre of the middle layers of your sponge cake with a pastry ring then fill the hole with jelly beans, smarties and other sweets. Put the top on and cover with icing as normal. When the birthday boy or girl cuts into the cake, the sweets should flood out giving everyone even more reason to celebrate.

**Buy some baking bling.** Go crazy with the edible glitter, shimmer sprays, neon sugar, popping candy, sweets, silver balls and sprinkles. Not only do they look brilliant but they will also hide any messy bits. Nice one.

**Remember that neatness isn't everything.** Looking colourful, fun and home-made with love is much more important than looking perfect.

I'D NEVER SPRAYED A CAKE BEFORE BUT IT WAS SO MUCH FUN AND LOOKED AMAZING! JUST MAKE SURE YOU DON'T SPRAY IT ALL OVER THE KITCHEN!

# INDEX

### V

### W

### Y

First published in Great Britain in 2017 by
Hodder & Stoughton

An Hachette UK company

11



A CIP catalogue record for this title is available from the British Library.

Hardback ISBN 978 1 473 65225 5
eBook ISBN 978 1 473 65226 2

Editorial Director: Nicky Ross
Project Editor: Laura Herring
Editorial Consultant: Camilla Stoddart
Design: Louise Leffler
Photography: Jemma Watts
Prop styling: Olivia Wardle
Food styling: Lizzie Kamenetzky
Illustrations: Sarah Leuzzi
Hair and make-up: Cassie Steward
Shoot Producer: Ruth Ferrier

Additional photography: Paul Ratcliffe, Colin Steele, Danny Rohrer and Archie Thomas.

Colour origination by Born
Printed and bound in Germany by Mohn Media GmbH

Hodder & Stoughton policy is to use papers that are natural, renewable and recyclable products and made from wood grown in sustainable forests. The logging and manufacturing processes are expected to conform to the environmental regulations of the country of origin.

Hodder & Stoughton Ltd
Carmelite House
50 Victoria Embankment
London
EC4Y 0DZ

www.hodder.co.uk

STUDIO RAMSAY

Matilda and the Ramsay bunch

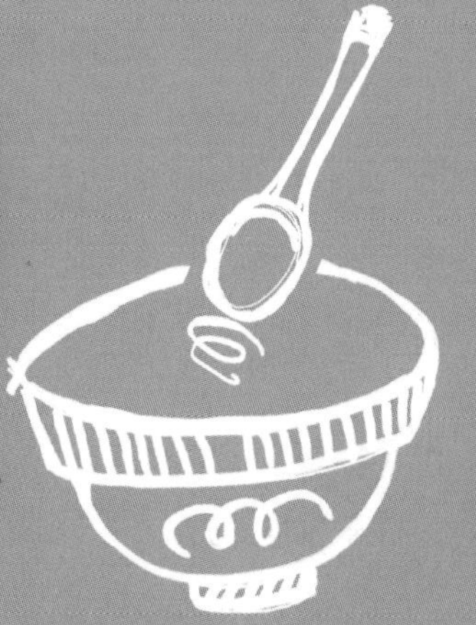

# THANKS YOU!

I was so excited when Hodder approached me to do this fabulous book alongside *Matilda and the Ramsay Bunch* – how cool! Everyone involved was super nice and we just had so much fun. I have a lot of thank yous, so here goes. Thank you to . . .

Nicky Ross – you believed in me and made me realise I could do this! Laura Herring managed the project effortlessly. Camilla Stoddart got all my ideas, methods and recipes down on paper – somehow! Louise Leffler designed the book and has made it look fabulous. Catriona Horne and Louise Swanell for getting out there and telling everyone about it.

Our photographer, Jemma Watts, was amazing, alongside prop stylist Olivia Wardle and food stylist Lizzie Kamenetzky. I LOVE the pictures of my food! And thanks to Cassie Steward for helping me look presentable for the front cover – you know how I shy away from being neat!

And then there is the team who make *Matilda and the Ramsay Bunch* for CBBC. Thank you all so much, it has always been so much fun and we got to do amazing things! There are too many names to mention across the three series but special thanks have to go to:
Paul Ratcliffe at Studio Ramsay who has known me since I was three years old! He has the patience of a saint and knows how to make me laugh . . . The amazing crew of camera and sound men: Danny Rohrer, Archie 'Moon' Thomas, Richard Hill, Kurt Lindquist, Steve Jones and Andy Boag. And the team on the other side – Colin Steele, Fiona Jones, Micah Moseley, Nora Cromwell, Caitlyn Mairs, Amy Franceschi, Ryan Newcombe, Holly Pickering, Mike Pipkin and Verity Sutton Barrow.

The home economists were also fab. Special thanks go to Mary 'Mezza' Keledjian, Avery Purcell, Sarah Durdin Robertson, Michaela Bowles and Whitney Webster who all agree that it is much more fun to work with me than Daddy . . .

Justin 'Mom' Mandell and Georgia 'George' McMillan – thank you both for working out all the timings and dates and keeping back enough time for me to have fun outside of school and homework. You both make it so much fun when we are meant to be serious. Thank you!!!

Thank you, also, to Hugh Lawton at the BBC.

And finally to the Bunch (ha ha!):
Thanks, Meggie, for always being the sensible voice and keeping the other two in line, and Holly, for helping with outfit choices and lending clothes and reminding me to always be prepared . . . Jack, for keeping us all on our toes with your crazy pranks and jokes and for making us laugh even though you drive us all crazy. Thank you, Rumpole, for occasionally getting out of bed to join us, and Bruno, the only 'person' I know who has more energy than Jack and me and can literally run circles around us all. And thanks to our cats, Ernie and Theodora, for being calm and serene at all times.

I need to say a special thank you to Nanny for always having her chicken soup at the ready when I feel tired and poorly . . . no one makes it like you – Dad's doesn't even come close!

Mum and Dad, thank you both for eating everything I cook. Daddy, I have learnt to take your comments with a pinch of salt – you will never just sit and enjoy food, there is always something to say . . . and your jokes (especially about boyfriends) NEVER get any funnier! Mummy, you taught me to listen, smile and ignore – it works every time.

So thank you to everyone involved! I have loved every moment of doing this so much and I hope you all have, too.